DEC 2009

W9-BNB-662

Cracking the
4th Grade
Reading & Math

A Parent's Guide to
Helping Your Child
Excel in School

By Christian Camozzi, Athlene Whyte-Smith,
and the Staff of the Princeton Review

Random House, Inc.
New York

RandomHouse.com

The Princeton Review is one of the nation's leaders in test preparation and a pioneer in the world of education. The Princeton Review offers a broad range of products and services to measurably improve academic performance for millions of students every year.

The Princeton Review is not affiliated with Princeton University or Educational Testing Service.

The Princeton Review, Inc.
2315 Broadway
New York, NY 10024
E-mail: booksupport@review.com

Published in the United States by Random House, Inc., New York

ISBN: 978-0-375-76605-3

Printed in the United States of America

9 8 7 6 5 4 3 2 1

First Edition

CREDITS

Series Editor: Casey Cornelius

Content Editor: Tony Mancus

Development Editor: Rachael Nevins

Production Editor: Melissa Lewis

Art Director: Neil McMahon

Senior Designer: Doug McGredy

Production Manager: Greta Blau

Production Coordinators: Leif Osgood and Elfranko Wessels

Illustrators: Doug McGredy, Tom Racine, and Tim Goldman

ACKNOWLEDGMENTS

This book would not have been possible without the contributions of a talented team of writers, editors, artists, and developers, who tackled this series with devotion and smarts.

CONTENTS

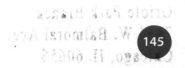

145 MATH

Introduction

You and Your Kid

Your job is to help your child excel in school. Everyone agrees that children bloom when their parents, family, friends, and neighbors nudge them to learn—from the Department of Education to the Parent Teacher Association, from research organizations known as "educational laboratories" to the local newspaper, from the National Endowment for the Arts to kids' shows on TV.

But state standards hardly make for enjoyable leisure reading, and plowing through reports on the best ways to teach math and reading can leave you with a headache, rubbing your temples. You're caught in the middle: you want to help your kid, but it's not always easy to know how.

That's where *Cracking the Fourth Grade* comes in. We identified the core skills that fourth graders need to know. Then, we put them together along with some helpful tips for you and fun activities for your kid. We built this book to be user-friendly, so you and your kid can fit in some quality time, even as you're juggling all your other parental responsibilities.

A Parent's Many Hats

As a parent, you're a cook, a chauffeur, a coach, an ally, and oh so many other things. So, keep it simple. Check out these ways you can use *Cracking the Fourth Grade* to get involved in your child's academic life.

Teacher. You taught your kid how to cross the street and tie his or her shoes. In addition, you may have worked to teach your child academic skills by reviewing definitions, helping your child memorize facts, and explaining concepts to your child. By doing so, you are modeling a great learning attitude and great study habits for your child. You are teaching him or her the value of school.

Nurturer. As a nurturer, you're always there to support your child through tough times, celebrate your child's successes, and give your child rules and limits. You encourage your child while holding high expectations. All of this can help your child feel safe and supported enough to face challenges and opportunities at school, such as tests, projects, new teachers, and so on.

Intermediary. You are your child's first representative in the world. You're the main go-between and communicator for your child (school-to-home and home-to-school).

Advocate. As an advocate, you can do many things: sit on advisory councils at school, assist in the classroom, join the PTA, volunteer in school programs, vote in school board elections, and argue for learning standards and approaches you believe in.

· · · · · · · · · · · · · · ● ●

Sometimes it's hard to know what to do, and it's easy to feel overwhelmed. But remember, it's not all on your shoulders. Research shows that family and close friends all have a huge effect on kids' academic success.

What's in This Book

The Skill
Each lesson targets a key fourth-grade skill. You and your kid can either work on all the lessons or pick and choose the lessons you want. If time is short, your kid can work on an activity without reviewing an entire lesson.

Just for You
Tips, advice, insight, and clues from parents and educators start here! Read this before diving into the rest of the lesson.

First Things First
This is the starting point for your kid in every lesson.

Supplies
Get your kid in the habit of gathering supplies before starting a lesson.

Jump Right In!
These are questions for your kid to complete independently. Give your kid as much time as he or she needs. But if your kid takes more than 30 minutes, consider the possibility that he or she may be having a hard time focusing, be unfamiliar with the skill, or have difficulty with the skill.

Range, Mode, and Mean

We live in a data-driven world filled with information about everything from how many people live in a certain area to who likes what flavor ice cream. We use data to make key decisions: what doctor to choose, what dinner to eat, how much to pay for things, and so on. While data is crucial, sometimes it seems our lives are dominated by data. We wonder what our kids' futures will be—strapping techno-gadgets to their brains, crunching numbers all the time, following streams of flowing data?

You know that your kids need to be comfortable understanding and using data. It's key for their lives today, and it's absolutely crucial for the future that they will be a part of creating.

By thinking about data in terms of range, mode, and mean, your child is starting to practice "viewing" data as a resource. The numbers aren't something to be memorized (there are too many numbers and sets of data in the world to memorize them all!)—the numbers are something to be understood. By having a chance to play around with range, mode, and mean, your kid can get more comfortable looking at data, pondering it, analyzing it, and even developing opinions about it.

First things first: Get a sense of what your kid already knows. Turn the page and tell your kid to Jump Right In!

Here's what you'll need for this lesson:
- *paper*
- *pencils*
- *timer or clock*

Jump Right In!

1. $3 \times 4 =$

A. 1

B. 7

C. 9

3. $6 \times 0 =$

A. 0

B. 5

Checking In
Check your kid's answers to the Jump Right In! questions. Whether your kid aced the Jump Right In! questions or had some trouble, here's stuff you can do to keep supporting your kid.

Checking In

Answers for page 13:

1. A

2. C

3. An A+ answer: "Primates are animals such as apes, gorillas, and mo
The story says that these animals are examples of primates and tha
their hands and feet to hold on to things."

4. An A+ answer: "Aquatic means something that lives in the water. T
says that fish and turtles are aquatic animals that live in the water

Did your child get the correct answers? If so, ask your child to point out the
clues in the story that showed the meaning of the words *watch* and *sign*.

Did your child get one of the answers wrong? If so, explain to your child that
watch and *sign* have more than one meaning. Review the answer choices to q
and 2 and talk about the various meanings of the words *watch* and *sign*.

Watch Out!

Watch Out!
These tips identify common pitfalls and help you help your child avoid them.

Sometimes fourth graders try to figure out a word's meaning by using the de
find the most interesting. For example, did your child select the wrong mea
word "watch" in question 1? Maybe he or she was thinking about watchi

What to Know...
Review these key skills, definitions, and examples with your kid. Questions and tips are provided so you and your kid can talk about the skills.

What to Know . . .

Kids use division all the time when they are sharing. Review these skills wit
child this way.

- **Equal groups** are groups that have the same number of items in th

- **Division** is an operation on two numbers that tells how many grou
It also tells how many items are in each group. The **division sign**

- The **quotient** is a number resulting from dividing a number by and
number. For example, in $24 \div 8 = 3$, the quotient is 3.

Fourth Graders Are...
Your child's natural stages of growth can play into academic success. These tips give you insider info on the developmental stages of your child and how to help your child through his or her transitions.

Fourth Graders Are...
Fourth graders like to search for things. Divide your home or yard into a "grid" and hide objects in each area. Give your kid coordinates and send him or her on a hunt to find those things!

On Your Way to an "A" Activities

{15 minutes}

Type: Art
Materials needed: Paper, scissors, a
Number of players: 2 or more

Play "Starry, starry night." Fold a piece of paper in ha out half of a star that includes part of the fold. When up the paper, you'll have a whole symmetrical star. T this time, fold the paper twice. Cut out part of a star both folds. Try making stars with many folds. Then h around your room!

 Study Right

Conducting research can help your child learn. Research symmetry Use a folder with two pockets. Label the left pocket "Asymmetrical" pocket "Symmetrical." Collect pictures as examples of asymmetrical shapes. Work with your child to identify the shapes and to put them pocket. Go through the pictures with your child and discuss why one symmetry while another does not.

Has your child breezed through the activities? If so, he or she can wor Your Head activity independently.

Using Your Head

{10 minutes}

*Grab a **pencil** and some **crayons** or **markers**!*

Read each problem. Decide if you have to add or su the word "add" or "subtract" to show what you nee Then, solve the problem.

How Does Your Kid Learn Best?

Did you know that your kid learns in a lot of different ways? When kids learn, they use their minds, their bodies, and their senses—sight, sound, taste, touch, and smell.

Some kids can succeed in any classroom, while others need specialized learning support, but all of them have strengths and weaknesses. Your kid can learn to rely on his or her strengths and then work on any weaknesses. This book is full of activities that address each of these learning styles.

Visually—Using Our Sense of Sight
Your kid may learn best by looking at pictures, outlines, maps, and such. Your kid may like to draw pictures or take notes.

Auditory—Using Our Sense of Sound
Your kid may learn best by listening to teachers speak, discussing with friends and classmates, and listening to music while studying. Your kid may like to tap a rhythm with his or her pen or pencil while studying.

Kinesthetic—Using Our Sense of Touch and Movement
Your kid may learn best by moving, taking action, or walking around.

How to Use Learning Styles

Talk with your child about his or her successes at school, home, or with hobbies. How did your child learn what he or she needed to succeed? Knowing how your child learns best can help you make the most of your child's natural strengths and work on your child's weaknesses.

Once you know how your child likes to learn, you can make sure your child includes those learning methods that work (especially when studying for important tests). You can also support your child as he or she tries out more challenging learning methods. In the long run, this will help your child become a well-rounded learner!

 *The Goal*

You know getting involved with your child's school experiences is the right decision. But here's a reminder of some of the rewards you may reap!

Research shows that getting involved in your kid's school experiences can result in:

- Increased academic performance

- Better behavior at school

- Increased academic motivation

- Better school attendance

And lest you think your kid reaps all the rewards, you might find that helping your child learn gives you:

- More info about your kid's school

- A greater sense of your own learning preferences

- More appreciation for all the work you did as a student

- A better relationship with your child's teacher and school staff

Want to Know More?

Check out these Web sites and organizations for more reading and math support.

Family Math and Matemática Para La Familia. If you want information about more effectively helping your child in mathematics, go to http://equals.lhs.berkeley.edu/.

MAPPS (Math and Parent Partnerships). If you want activities and mini-courses to learn about becoming more engaged in your child's school mathematics program, go to http://math.arizona.edu/~mapps/.

National Parent School Partnership (PSP) Program. If you want to better understand parental rights, the structure of schools, and how to enhance parent/teacher conferences, go to www.maldef.org/psp.

Parent Information and Resource Centers (PIRCs). If you want information about your rights under the No Child Left Behind Act as well as training, advocates, or other assistance, go to www.ed.gov/programs/pirc/index.html.

Parents for Public Schools. If you want to find out about chapters of parents working together to advocate for school improvement, go to www.parents4publicschools.com.

PTA (Parent Teacher Association). If you want to connect with other parents involved in local schools, go to www.pta.org.

Parent Training and Information Centers. If you want to find out about education and services to assist a child with disabilities, go to www.taalliance.org/centers/index.htm.

PESA (Parent Expectations Support Achievement). If you want techniques for improving your child's academic achievement, go to http://streamer.lacoe.edu/pesa/.

PIQE (Parent Institute for Quality Education). If you want to learn about how to motivate your child in school, develop a home learning environment, work with the school system, or prepare for college, go to www.pique.org.

Reading Is Fundamental. If you want help with supporting your child's reading and learning, go to www.rif.org.

Reading

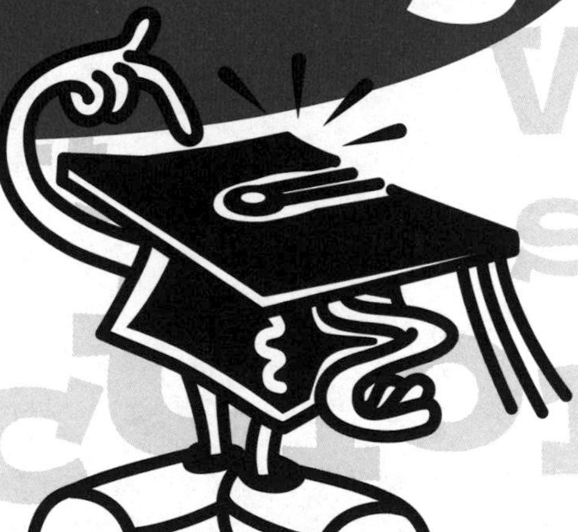

Using Context

In grade 4, kids are really beginning to grow as readers. They might not even notice how much reading they do each day. They read signs in stores, directions on games, and stories at school. All of this reading helps them sharpen their comprehension skills and build their vocabularies.

Every day, they come across new words—from *hazard* to *polka dot* and *concrete* to *pyramid*. They also come across familiar words used in new ways. For example, they probably know that a *kid* is a child, but they may not know that it is also a young goat. These are multiple-meaning words.

Unfamiliar words are best decoded using context clues. Sometimes it can be a challenge to find clues, and sometimes children use the details they find the most interesting to try to determine the meaning of a word, even when those details are unrelated. To answer questions involving the meaning of words, your fourth grader must be able to identify appropriate context clues and use them correctly.

First things first: Get a sense of what your kid already knows. Turn the page and tell your kid to Jump Right In!

Here's what you'll need for this lesson:
- paper and pencils
- markers or crayons
- dictionary

 **Jump Right In!**

Anna and Zack

Anna and Zack seemed so different. Anna was born in a small town in Montana, loved math, and ate peanut butter for breakfast. She wore an orange hat to school every day and had a pet hamster named Milkshake.

Zack was born in New York City and preferred poetry. He wore <u>plain</u> white shirts and brown shoes, and liked to read in the morning. He often fed a squirrel that lived in a pine tree next door.

Anna and Zack were different, but they were good friends. They both lived in Portland, Maine, and went to the same school. They played dodgeball during recess and sat next to each other during lunch.

"Anna is fun," said Zack. "She and I both play with a gray cat that lives near our school. Anna is better at soccer than I am; she hardly ever <u>trips</u>. But I'm better at checkers than she is. We seem to like the same things."

This made Anna smile. "Zack is cool," she said, twisting on her heel. "He's always in a good mood, and he's nice to everyone. Plus, he can play the guitar as well as our music teacher."

Zack planned to try out for the school play the following week. "I have to stay an hour after school every day for <u>rehearsal</u>," he said. "My parents said it's okay. I hope Anna tries out too."

"I might, but I'm scared to be on stage in front of everyone. My mom says I have stage fright," she said, as she pulled her hat down over her forehead.

"Most people do," Zack said. "But we can be nervous together!"

Cracking the Fourth Grade

1. In the second paragraph, the passage says that Zack wears plain white shirts. What does the word *plain* mean?

　　A. clean

　　B. dark

　　C. simple

　　D. free

2. Zack says that Anna hardly ever trips while playing soccer. What does the word *trip* mean in this context?

　　A. to go on vacation

　　B. to fall down

　　C. to score

　　D. to skip

3. Zack says that if he is in the play, he will have to stay after school for rehearsal. Write what the word *rehearsal* means.

_____

_____

_____

4. What context clues from the passage did you use to prepare your answer to question 3?

_____

_____

_____

Excellent Job!

 **Checking In**

Ⓐ Answers for page 13:

1. C

2. B

3. An A+ answer: "A rehearsal is a practice for a performance that will happen later."

4. An A+ answer: "In the passage, Zack says that he would have to go to rehearsal every day after school if he is in the play. This tells us that rehearsal will prepare him for the performance. It is like practice in a sport."

If your child chose the correct answers, make sure that he or she used context clues. You might ask your child to underline the details that were important.

If your child answered any of the questions incorrectly, try to figure out why. You might ask, "What can you use to help you define the word *rehearsal* in the story?" Help your child find useful context clues by noting information around the word *rehearsal* that would help to define it, like the fact that Zack is trying out for the play. Then, try answering the questions again as a team.

 **Watch Out!**

Sometimes fourth graders think that context clues have to be located near the word they're trying to figure out, but this isn't always the case. For example, at the beginning of the passage, we learn that Anna and Zack seemed different. We find out that Anna wears an orange hat. Zack, meanwhile, wears plain white shirts. Their clothes are different, and if Anna's clothes are brightly colored, this is another clue to the meaning of *plain*. In this case, the clue is in another paragraph. Encourage your child to look for clues throughout the passage.

What to Know...

Your kid comes across new words every day.

Review these skills with your child this way:

- **Context clues** are words, phrases, and information that surround a word in a passage that help you figure out the meaning of the word.
- **Multiple-meaning words** are words that have several different meanings depending on how they are used in a sentence.

Your child might see the following poster at school.

Do You Want to Try Out for the School Play?

If only I could sleep...

Auditions for *The Princess and the Pea* are this Friday at 3 P.M. in the main auditorium.

See Mr. Monzi in room 134 for more information.

Ask your child to circle any new words in the poster. These might include *auditions* and *auditorium*. Ask, "What context clues can help you figure out the meanings of these words?" Also, point out that the word *play* can have more than one meaning.

 *Checking In*

Your child should be able to determine that:

- Auditions are when you try out for a play.
- An auditorium is a room in which an audition might happen.

Ask your child to expand these definitions. You might ask:

- What does an auditorium look like, and why would an audition take place there?

Type: Arts and Crafts
Materials needed: paper, markers or crayons
Number of players: 2 or more

Think of someone interesting, but don't say the person's name out loud. This person might be someone you saw on television or met in real life. Now, draw a simple stick figure. Add details to the drawing that reveal who this person is. Add these details one by one. After you add each detail, ask your partner to guess who this person is. Notice that the details you add are context clues. They tell people who this person is.

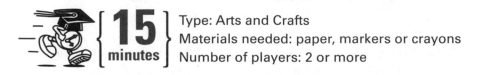

Type: Active
Materials needed: none
Number of players: 2

Think of a word that has more than one meaning. You might choose a word like *bark*. This describes the noise that a dog makes, but it also describes the outer layer of a tree. Have your partner tell you all of the word's meanings. You can take turns coming up with multiple-meaning words.

Fourth Graders Are...

Some fourth graders might be embarrassed when they don't know the meaning of a word. Tell your child that everyone encounters new words—even you. Encourage your child to be excited to find out what new words mean. If there aren't any context clues, your child can use a dictionary. Challenge each other to use new words in conversation.

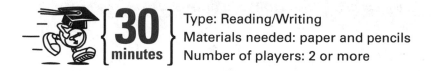

Type: Reading/Writing
Materials needed: paper and pencils
Number of players: 2 or more

Ask a parent to give you a list of new words. These must be new words for everyone in the game. Your parent might give you three words or five words. It's up to you. Your parent should use each word in a sentence. For example, your parent might choose the word *precious* and use it in a sentence like this, "Grandma always kept her precious stones locked away in a safe place." Or a word like *gradually* in a sentence like, "During springtime, the days gradually grow longer." Then, the players take turns trying to define the words. Whoever gets the definition right wins. Then, you should take turns coming up with sentences using these words. Each sentence you write should build on the sentence that comes before it. This will allow you to create a fun story. If there are two players and three new words, your story will have six sentences. You might even start keeping your own dictionary with the words you learn.

 **Study Right**

Encourage your child to keep a list of new words and their meanings. You can make this fun. For example, the list might be written with colorful markers, or you might give your child a special notebook in which to write these new words. You also might keep the list on your refrigerator at home. This will help your child build a strong vocabulary. It will also help reinforce the meanings of these words with your child.

Using Your Head

*Grab a **pencil**!*

Zack and Anna are writing essays about the school play for their English class. Their teacher tells them that they each have to use a new word. Zack chooses the word *friendly*, which means nice, or easy to get along with. Anna chooses the word *challenging*, which means hard or difficult. Their teacher asks them to include context clues to help their classmates determine the meanings of these words.

1. Help Zack out. Write a sentence that uses the word *friendly*. In your sentence, be sure to include enough context clues so his classmates can figure out the meaning of the word.

_____

_____

_____

2. Now, help Anna. Write a sentence that uses the word *challenging*. In your sentence, make sure that you include enough context clues so her classmates can figure out the meaning of the word.

_____

_____

_____

Before Reading

In grade 4, kids begin to see themselves as readers—not only as readers in school, but as readers in the world. Some kids think the purpose for reading can be determined only by the teacher or that reading is simply a way to get information. However, you know that people read things for many reasons—for fun, to figure out how to make a cake, or even to find out where Walla Walla is.

Good readers understand that reading is an active process. They participate in that process by knowing why they are reading, using information they have, and thinking about what might happen next. To become an active reader, your kid needs a plan for using his or her prior knowledge, without having that knowledge overshadow the new information that's being presented by the text.

To become a strong reader with good comprehension skills, your fourth grader needs to determine why he or she is reading, as well as how to use the information from the text to make predictions.

First things first: Get a sense of what your kid already knows. Turn the page and tell your kid to Jump Right In!

Here's what you'll need for this lesson:
- a newspaper with a photo of a famous person
- several reading materials, such as magazines, brochures, take-out menus, recipes, or anything else with words on it
- a short story
- paper and pencils

Jump Right In!

Love the Earth!

We all need to take care of the planet we share. We need to make sure that the Earth is around for people in the future. Let's all do our part!

Here are some simple things you can do:

- Take shorter showers or use less water in your bath. This will save water.
- Recycle your bottles, cans, and paper. Ask your parents to help you figure out how to do this.
- Turn the lights off when you leave a room. This will save electricity.
- Be careful with paper. Use both sides of each sheet of paper. Use leftover sheets of paper for notes or letters. This will help save trees.
- If possible, hang your clothes to dry outside. A dryer uses a lot of electricity. This will help you cut down on the amount of electricity you use.
- Don't litter. If you have something that you need to throw away, wait until you are near a trash can. Never throw it on the ground. The trash can wind up in our lakes, rivers, or oceans.
- Plant a tree or flowers. Ask your parents to help you. If you can't do this at home, think about doing it at your grandparents' home, your school, or at a local park. Trees provide shade on hot days, and both trees and flowers even clean the air we all breathe.

1. Someone might read this passage

    A. to find a recycling center near his or her school

    B. to enjoy a story about trees and flowers

    C. to learn about how to care for the planet

    D. to find out how electricity works

2. If the author wrote more, what else might the author ask you to do?

    A. Leave your television on when you leave the house.

    B. Wash your towels every day.

    C. Have your parents drive you to school each morning.

    D. Turn the water off as you brush your teeth.

3. What will using both sides of a sheet of paper do?

    _____

    _____

    _____

4. Have you learned about caring for the Earth before? If so, when? What did you learn?

    _____

    _____

    _____

Excellent Job!

 *Checking In*

1. C
2. D
3. An A+ answer: "If you use both sides of a piece of paper, you use less of the Earth's resources. This means the Earth will have more resources for the future."
4. An A+ answer: "I learned about caring for the Earth from Saturday morning cartoons. I learned that people should try to use their cars less to help reduce pollution."

If your child answered correctly, ask, "What information in the passage did you use to choose your answers?" Ask your child to write his or her reasons for choosing the correct answers in the margins and to underline the words in the passage that helped him or her identify those answers.

If your child answered incorrectly, ask, "What were your reasons for choosing that answer?" Make sure you understand how your child arrived at the incorrect answer. If your child used prior knowledge that is not appropriate for this question, explain why the information is inappropriate and ask him or her to try again.

 *Watch Out!*

Sometimes it's good for fourth graders to make their reading relevant by accessing knowledge that they already have about a particular topic. For example, with question 4, your child could have learned about caring for the Earth from many different places, such as school or television or friends or even other reading material. And if your kid does have prior knowledge about a particular topic, that knowledge ought to help your child figure out whatever it is he or she is reading. It doesn't hurt to push your child to look into things that he or she seems interested in. Kids at this age are often tremendously curious, and children can be encouraged to indulge their curiosity through reading. Provide your kid with the opportunity to read for enjoyment as well as to find out new things.

What to Know...

When your kid sits down to read, how does she prepare herself? There are many things your kid can do to prepare to read and to help herself understand a passage while she is reading.

Review these skills with your child this way:

- **Prior knowledge** is any relevant information we have before we begin reading.

- A **prediction** is an idea or thought about the future.

- Strong readers often set a **purpose** for reading—they know if they are reading to **get information** or to **have fun**. To get information, people might read newspapers, instruction manuals, editorials, essays, dictionaries, cookbooks, and other texts. To have fun, people might read poems, novels, plays, short stories, and other texts.

You and your child might see a sign like this when visiting a recycling center.

Ask your kid, "What do you know about recycling or recycling centers?" Then, ask your child, "If we were going to the recycling center, what might we do after seeing this sign?" Then, ask your child if he would read the sign for fun or to get information.

 *Checking In*

When correctly using prior knowledge, your kid might say:

- I've never been to a recycling center, but I know that people recycle to help the Earth.

- Our local recycling center takes only newspaper, but this one takes newspaper, cans, and bottles.

Children struggle when they use prior knowledge instead of details in a text:

- Our local recycling center takes only newspapers, so I think this sign is wrong.

- Our old cans and bottles are dirty, so no one would want them.

Most kids can use information to make predictions:

- The recycling center would like our old copies of *Time* magazine.

- If we go later than 6 p.m., the center will be closed.

Most kids can use information to set a purpose:

- I would read this sign because I want to get information about how to recycle things at the recycling center.

Fourth Graders Are...

Fourth graders sometimes assume information they have is the only information there is. It can be fun to surprise your child with facts that might not fit with what he or she already knows. You might ask, "Do you think Grandma likes to dance?" If your child says no, you might respond, "Grandma won a jitterbug contest when she was younger." This will help your child understand how prior information can lead to incorrect predictions.

On Your Way to an "A" Activities

{15 minutes}

Type: Reading/Writing
Materials needed: a newspaper with a photo of a famous person
Number of players: 2

Be a fortune teller! Have one player silently read the newspaper article that goes with the photo. That player should keep the details of the story to himself or herself. The player who reads the story should show the other person the photo and give a very general idea of what the story is about. The player who did not read the story should write a paragraph that predicts what the story says. How close are the two stories? The player who wrote the paragraph should consider the prior information that he or she used. Were the predictions correct?

{15 minutes}

Type: Speaking/Listening
Materials needed: reading materials, such as a newspaper, magazine, brochures, take-out menus, bus schedules, novels, plays, recipes, directions on the side of a box, and so on
Number of players: 2

Spread the reading materials out all over the room. Have one player stand in the center so he or she can see all of the materials at once. That player points to each item, one by one. For each, he or she asks if it would be read to get information or to have fun. After going over about half of the materials, you should switch positions. After all of the materials are identified, you can discuss several articles in each magazine and newspaper. Notice how different your answers are for each type of reading material. How is your answer for a recipe different from your answer for a novel?

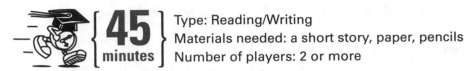

Type: Reading/Writing
Materials needed: a short story, paper, pencils
Number of players: 2 or more

Read the first half of a short story. Stop at the halfway point and predict what will happen in the rest of the story. Write a paragraph to describe your prediction. Have fun with it. If you want, draw a picture to accompany your story. Then, finish reading the story. Did you correctly predict the ending? What information did you use to make your predictions? Did you use prior information? If so, was it incorrect?

Study Right

Show your child how to set a purpose when reading. You can do this with a variety of texts. If you are reading a recipe, you could point out that you are reading the recipe to figure out how to make a particular dish. Or, if you are reading directions on the side of a box, you might point out that you want to make sure you do something correctly. If you are reading a novel, you can explain that you are doing it for pleasure and what kind of pleasure this type of reading produces. This will help your child understand the variety of texts that are out there, as well as the range of reasons why we read things. After a week or so, turn the tables on your child. Encourage your kid to tell you why he or she is reading something, such as a poster or a letter.

Using Your Head

{10} minutes

*Grab a **pencil**!*

Juan wrote the following paragraph for school. Read Juan's paragraph. Then, answer the questions that follow.

Little Chores That Help

I do a lot of little things to help save our planet. When I brush my teeth in the morning, I always turn the water off. I think about all the fish smiling while I'm brushing. They'll still have some water to swim in, even if it's just a tiny bit more. When my family and I went on a picnic in the summer, my parents wanted to throw away their plastic forks and cups, but I wouldn't let them. They thought I was being a pain, but it doesn't really take much time or effort to take the forks and cups home and wash them. This way we can use them again, and somebody else won't have to carry around so much trash when they clean up the park. I also reuse scraps of paper whenever I can. For example, when I needed to write a letter to my teacher about trying to get the school to recycle, I wrote it on the back of an ingredient list from a tin can. I hope she could still read it. These things may seem small, but I think they add up, especially if I do them every day for the rest of my life. Every little bit helps, you know.

1. The title of this passage is "Little Chores That Help." What do you already know about chores? And how do Juan's chores help?

   _____

   _____

2. Juan wants to make a list of things he needs to do over the weekend. He will most likely write this list on

   A. a new page in his notebook

   B. the back of an old flyer from school

   C. a clean sheet of paper

Answers: 1. I know that chores are work of some kind, like washing dishes and taking out the trash. The chores that Juan does help the earth. 2. B

During Reading: Connections

Fourth graders are learning how to process their thoughts, feelings, and opinions as they read. They are continuing to develop their sense of outside issues, as well as their ability to articulate their thoughts and feelings about these issues. The combination of learning so much about the world and becoming aware of internal feelings can sometimes be overwhelming.

Kids sometimes make connections based on whatever issue feels most important in their personal lives at the moment. For example, if a child is newly aware that people live in poverty, he or she might focus on this issue in a character's life. This kind of connection is good. It shows that your child is feeling and understanding the text.

To tackle questions that require kids to start seeing the links between what they are reading and their own experiences, as well as what is going on in the world, your fourth grader needs to be able to make accurate and appropriate connections.

First things first: Get a sense of what your kid already knows. Turn the page and tell your kid to Jump Right In!

Here's what you'll need for this lesson:

- *a newspaper, magazine, or book*
- *any art supplies you have*
- *paper*
- *pencils*
- *crayons*

 **Jump Right In!**

An Amazing Animal

What do you think is the fastest animal on land? Some people might think it is a horse or a wolf. Others might say it is a zebra or a giraffe, but none of those animals can keep up with a cheetah. The cheetah is the fastest animal on the planet.

A cheetah is a spotted cat. It can run more than 70 miles per hour. That's faster than your parents drive on the freeway! Humans are much slower. The athletes you see in the Olympics can run only about 23 miles per hour.

Cheetahs eat meat. They hunt other animals, such as antelope, deer, or even rabbits. They hunt mainly in the morning and late afternoon. This is when the Sun's heat is less strong. They sneak up on these animals. They get as close as possible before chasing them down.

About 100 years ago, cheetahs lived all over Africa. They also lived in many parts of Asia. Today, they live mainly in the southern parts of Africa.

Cheetahs have beautiful spots. In the past, clothing made out of cheetah fur was seen as showing the power and status of whomever owned such a piece of clothing.

Cheetahs prefer to live in areas that have tall grass, large plants, and bushes. These things allow them to hide. They want to stay away from people who might want to hunt *them*!

Cheetahs are beautiful. It is amazing to watch a cheetah run at full speed. It can take your breath away!

1. Read this excerpt from a novel:

When I was 11, my family moved to Africa. I was scared about moving so far. But I knew we had to move. My mom worked to help cheetahs survive. Even though I was scared, I was excited to help these amazing animals.

Both passages say that cheetahs are:

A. fast

B. amazing

C. beautiful

D. furry

2. How do you feel about cheetahs?

_____

_____

3. About 100 years ago, there were many more cheetahs than there are now. What information in the passage could explain why there are so few cheetahs now?

_____

_____

Excellent Job!

 *Checking In*

Ⓐ Answers for page 31:

    1. B

    2. An A+ answer: "I think cheetahs are scary, but they're beautiful. And they're super fast."

    3. An A+ answer: "People might want to hunt cheetahs because they might want the cheetah's skin."

If your child answered correctly, ask, "Have you read anything else about cheetahs or seen cheetahs on TV or in movies? If so, when? Were you reminded of anything by this passage?"

If your child answered incorrectly, review her answers. For example, if your child answered question 1 incorrectly, your child may have picked the answer that shows how she feels about cheetahs, not how the two passages describe cheetahs. Ask your child, "Which answer choice shows how the author of "An Amazing Animal" feels about cheetahs? Do any of these answer choices also show how the person who moved to Africa felt about cheetahs?" Explain to your child that question 1 asked her to make a connection between two different passages, so she needs to use the details in those passages. Point out that question 2 asks her to make a connection between her own feelings and the passage, so she can use details from the passage as well as her own thoughts and feelings.

 *Watch Out!*

Sometimes fourth graders base their answers on their feelings while dismissing information in passages. For example, if your kid is afraid of big cats, she might say that people hunt cheetahs because they are dangerous to people and not notice the information about people wearing clothing made from cheetah fur. Remind your child that the correct answer to a test question must be based on information from the passage.

What to Know...

When reading comic books, completing homework, and even watching the news, your child is making text-to-self connections, text-to-world connections, and text-to-text connections.

Review these skills with your child this way:

- **Text-to-self connections.** Strong readers build links and relationships between the text and their everyday lives and personal experiences.

- **Text-to-world connections.** Strong readers build links and relationships between the text and the world. They link details from the text with things they see in the world and events going on in the world.

- **Text-to-text connections.** Strong readers build links and relationships between different parts of a text. For example, they link details from the beginning of a text to the end of a text. Strong readers also build links and relationships between different texts, like from one story to another story, or from an article to visual media (such as a movie or a picture, etc.).

Your kid might draw connections between a cheetah and your house cat because of how cheetahs and cats look and act. She may even develop an interest in taking photos of the cat because of this. This shows that your child is starting to apply what she is seeing and reading to her life, or making text-to-self connections.

 *Study Right*

Encourage your kid to draw connections between the subject of a text and other things. Before reading, ask your kid to consider his or her feelings, thoughts, or ideas about the subject. Ask where these ideas came from, and if he or she learned about the subject somewhere else. These questions will help your child create connections between the text and his or her experience as well as the outside world.

Your kid may read and view several things about cheetahs and make connections between these things. For example. you and your child might come across the following blurb in a television schedule and want to watch the program.

The World's Wild Animals: Cheetahs

This episode follows the life of a small group of cheetahs in the wild. Watch them hunt for food, play in the sun, and sleep in the shade. Our cameras will take you closer than you have ever been before.

Ask your child to describe what you two might see on this show. What animals might the cheetahs hunt? Where might these cheetahs live?

Most kids can draw connections between what they've read and this television program:

- The cheetahs might hunt zebra, antelope, or rabbit.
- The cheetahs might live in the southern part of Africa.

Kids struggle when they draw inaccurate connections between texts:

- The cheetahs might hunt humans.
- The cheetahs might live in a park in the United States.

 *Checking In*

In answering question 3 on page 31, your kid should have started to think about the position of cheetahs over time. This sets his reading into a much larger picture. In order to answer that question correctly, he will have to rely on making text-to-world connections and seeing the reduced number of cheetahs in the wild as a product of something that is happening beyond the text. It's something that's in the actual world that surrounds him.

On Your Way to an "A" Activities

Type: Arts/Crafts

Materials needed: something to read such as a newspaper, magazine, or book, and art supplies such as markers, crayons, construction paper, pipe cleaners, sparkles, glue, tape

Number of players: 2

Find something interesting to read. You might choose an article in a magazine or newspaper, a novel, a play, or a poem. Read the text and pay close attention to your feelings. How does it make you feel? Use the art supplies to express your thoughts and feelings.

Type: Speaking/Listening

Materials needed: a newspaper

Number of players: 2 or more

Choose a story about people who live in another country. Read the story carefully. What did you learn about these people's lives? How are these people's lives different from your own? Think about how you spend your day. Then, think about how someone in that country might spend the day. Make a chart that shows the comparisons between your everyday activities and those of a person in another country.

Feel free to take any of the activities described in this book outside, if possible. You might want to invite other kids to join in. This will make the activity even more fun for your child. You might take the activity to a park, a zoo, or even the lawn outside your local library.

Has your child breezed through the activities? If so, he or she can work on this Using Your Head activity independently.

Using Your Head

*Grab some **paper**, a **pencil**, and some **crayons**!*

You can also make connections between pictures and passages. Read "An Amazing Animal" again. Then, look at the pictures and answer the questions.

1. A cheetah would most likely eat the

   _____.

2. Color the things in the picture that also are mentioned in "An Amazing Animal."

Answers: 1. rabbit; 2. Color in the cheetah, the rabbit, the grasses, and the sun.

During Reading: Checking Understanding

As kids read more complicated texts, they're likely to find themselves confused. "Who is she?" they might ask, when a character reenters a story. Confusion is a natural part of reading. What's important, though, is how they respond to this confusion. You need to help your kid develop the tools to clarify any misunderstandings.

Fourth graders sometimes internalize their confusion as a reflection of their abilities. They might say, "I'll never get this" or "This is boring." Sometimes they're embarrassed to say when they are confused. They also tend to speed through their work. They want to be the first to say, "Finished," as the class reads a passage. But haste produces sloppy reading. They need to take the time to grasp what they read.

Your fourth grader needs to be able to envision the story as he or she reads it, understand the information in it, and ask questions to clear up any confusion.

First things first: Get a sense of what your kid already knows. Turn the page and tell your kid to Jump Right In!

Here's what you'll need for this lesson:
- paper and pencils
- art supplies, such as markers, crayons, glitter, sparkles, and glue
- a story, poem, or article

 **Jump Right In!**

Meet My Four Friends

Abel adores apples,
always wears a belt,
and answers e-mails right away.
He reads books about Alaska,
thinks eggs are awful,
and aces algebra.
He's A-OK.

Gillian gets grumpy
when things don't go her way.
But she's good at golf,
loves the Go-Gos,
and gives her dog Gigi
vegetables.
She's great.

Nate is as neat as a pin,
never nods off in class,
but knows nothing about Norway.
He notices when Nan
reads a new novel
in November.
He's super nice.

Wanda wonders why
the world is round
and where walruses wander.
She wears white in winter
and wishes we all wrote
with pink ink.
She's wacky.

These are my four friends. Who's your favorite?

1. Which friend does <u>not</u> like eggs?
   A. Abel
   B. Gillian
   C. Nate
   D. Wanda

2. Which friend thinks people should write with pink ink?
   A. Abel
   B. Gillian
   C. Nate
   D. Wanda

3. Try to picture Nate in your mind. What does he look like? Draw a picture or describe him in detail.

   _____

   _____

4. Imagine that Gillian enters a contest but does not win. How do you think she reacts? Be sure to use information from the poem to support your answer.

   _____

   _____

   _____

Excellent Job!

 *Checking In*

ⒶAnswers for page 39:

1. A

2. D

3. An A+ answer: "Nate's a very neat person. His clothes are sparkling and all tucked in."

4. An A+ answer: "I think she is not happy about the contest. She is probably in a bad mood since she did not win."

If your child answered correctly, you could ask, "Who was your favorite character from the poem?" Ask your kid to underline the information that he or she was drawn to about this character. Have your child draw a picture of this character.

If your child answered incorrectly, you could ask, "Why did you pick that answer?" If your child guessed, you might say, "It's important to base your answer on information you are given. If you're not sure of the answer, try going back to the poem." Then read it over together, stopping to discuss important information. For example, in question 2, you can point out that in the last stanza the poem mentions Wanda's interest in pink ink.

 *Watch Out!*

Sometimes fourth graders dismiss their confusion as they read. They might think that if they continue to read, it will clear up. But sometimes this doesn't happen. Encourage your child to get in the habit of identifying when he is confused. Then, if he isn't clear after reading another line or two, your child should stop and resolve the confusion. Once your child fels his confusion is resolved, tell him to reread the section that was confusing to be absolutely sure that he now understands everything clearly. When your kid is reading a particularly confusing passage, encourage him to take notes on a separate sheet of paper. You might get your child a special pen and reading journal for this purpose—to make it seem more fun. Don't be surprised if your kid is quick to go along with this idea—kids this age love to organize things and create order!

What to Know...

Your child is doing more and more reading at this age. Quantity is important—but so is the quality of his or her reading skills. You want to make sure that your child grasps the information he or she is given.

Review these skills with your child this way:

- **Picture the story.** Strong readers develop their comprehension by picturing the story (imagining the details and the actions) as they read.

- **Check understanding and clear up confusion.** Strong readers check their understanding—they stop and take moments to make sure they understood what they have just read. They ask themselves questions like, "What does that mean?"; "Do I know what is going on?"; or "What just happened?"

- **Ask questions.** Strong readers are curious and ask questions as they read. They ask questions about the details, they wonder about the story, and they are curious about what they are reading.

You and your child might see a poster like this in your neighborhood.

Ask your child to read the poster very carefully, then to look away. To determine how well he or she took in the information from the poster, you might ask, "What color are the cat's eyes? What does the cat's tail look like?"

 *Checking In*

Most kids should be able to recall information from the poster:

- The cat's eyes are green.
- The cat is a boy with a fluffy tail.

Some children might mix some of the details up in their heads:

- There are three colors mentioned in the poster, but which one describes the cat's eyes?
- The poster says the cat's hair is long. Does that describe the cat's tail?

 *Study Right*

Encourage your child to take breaks in his or her reading to make sure that everything is clear. Your child might stop at the end of each paragraph and ask himself if he can explain what he's just read to someone else. You might have him do this with some reading materials around the house to get him in the habit. If your kid can't give you a decent account of what he's read, then encourage him to go back and reread the page, noting important information.

On Your Way to an "A" Activities

30 minutes

Type: Arts and Crafts
Materials needed: art supplies, paper
Number of players: 2 or more

Play Cops and Robbers. One player should imagine seeing a robber. This player should imagine the robber and describe the robber to the other player. The other player is the cop who draws the robber based on the descriptions. The cop shouldn't show the picture to the other player until it's done. Then, all the players should look at the picture. Does the robber in the picture look like how the first player imagined and described the robber? Switch roles and play again.

45 minutes

Type: Game/Competitive
Materials needed: a story, poem, or article
Number of players: 2

Pretend you are on a game show! Everyone in the game should read the story, poem, or article. Then, each player should come up with a list of questions. These questions should test your understanding of what you just read. Take turns asking a question. Whoever misses the fewest questions wins! You might give a fun prize to the winner.

Has your child breezed through the activities? If so, he or she can work on this Using Your Head activity independently.

Using Your Head

[**30** minutes]

*Grab a **pencil** and **some paper**!*

In the poem, "Meet My Four Friends," you met Nate, Abel, Gillian, and Wanda. You learned that Nate knows nothing about Norway. Do you have questions about Norway?

You can help Nate out. Do some research on Norway. You can read an encyclopedia entry on the country, or you can go on the Internet. After you've done some research, answer the questions about Norway.

1. What continent is Norway in? What does the country look like on a map? Does it border any other countries?

   _____

2. To help picture the other characters in the poem, draw portraits of Gillian, Wanda, and Abel on separate pieces of paper, using details from the poem.

Answers: 1. Norway is in Europe. It looks very long on a map. The top of the country is narrow, but the bottom is wider. It borders Sweden. 2. Pictures of 3 characters with proper details used for each.

After Reading

For fourth graders, the terms *summary* and *detail* are most likely familiar, but they probably don't use them outside of their reading class. Your kid may not realize how often she comes across—and relies on—summaries. On the back of a DVD, for example, she will find a paragraph explaining what the movie's about, and it may determine whether or not she'll watch it.

In summarizing a text, kids this age might be most drawn to details that seem interesting or exciting but are not necessarily important. They might be drawn to a summary that offers an explanation or interpretation but excludes the most important details from the text. You need to help them determine which details are essential and which are not. This will help them create strong summaries.

First things first: Get a sense of what your kid already knows. Turn the page and tell your kid to Jump Right In!

Here's what you'll need for this lesson:
- art supplies, such as markers and crayons
- a newspaper
- pencils and paper

 **Jump Right In!**

The Art Contest

Jade stood before her class, beaming. Mr. Kolling patted her on the back. "Congratulations," he said. "Your picture won first prize in the art contest."

Mr. Kolling pinned a red ribbon to Jade's shirt and handed her a beautiful certificate. "First prize," it read, the gold letters shining in the light: "Jade Song."

"Thank you, Mr. Kolling," Jade said. She was proud of her drawing, but she felt shy. She tried to hide behind the giant flag that stood in the corner of the classroom.

"You also won this box of art supplies," Mr. Kolling added, handing Jade a big white box. "You can use them to create more masterpieces."

Jade laughed. She noticed Mark in the second row. Jade thought about how he had won second place. He seemed a little sad. His smile wasn't as big as the other students'. "Second place is still great," she thought to herself.

At home that evening, Jade's parents made her favorite food for dinner. She was still smiling from her big win at school as she ate the delicious tacos.

After dinner, Jade studied her drawing in her bedroom. On the back, Mr. Kolling had written two numbers in green ink. One was for creativity, the other was for skill: 52 and 44. Her total score appeared in giant red: 98.

Jade studied the numbers some more—and made a scary discovery. "Those two numbers add up to only 96!" she gasped.

She knew that Mark had received a score of 97. "I got second place," she whispered. "Not first."

Jade felt confused. "What should I do?" she asked herself over and over. She thought about Mark. She thought about her first prize ribbon. She thought about how it felt to win.

1. Mr. Kolling judged the students' work based on
   A. effort and achievement
   B. size and shape
   C. beauty and color
   D. creativity and skill

2. Which of these titles best summarizes the passage?
   A. How to Draw Like an Artist
   B. Jade's Masterpiece
   C. Art Contest Mix-up
   D. Mr. Kolling and His Class

3. Reread the first two paragraphs of the story. Try to summarize those two paragraphs in one sentence.

   _____

   _____

4. Write a brief summary of the story. Keep your answer to one or two sentences.

   _____

   _____

Excellent Job!

 *Checking In*

Answers for page 47:

1. D

2. C

3. An A+ answer: "Mr. Kolling announced that Jade won the school's art contest."

4. An A+ answer: "Jade wins her school's art contest but discovers that Mr. Kolling made a mistake in scoring her drawing."

Did your child pick the correct answers? If so, tell your child to underline the details that he or she used.

Did your child miss any of the questions? If so, explain to your child that a summary includes the most important details. Review the answer choices for question 2. Explain that the first answer sounds like the story would be instructive. While it does begin to teach a lesson, it certainly doesn't inform the reader how to draw. Only the third answer wholly sums up the story because it relies on all of the important details. If your kid picked the second answer, you could say, "That's a good try, but was Jade's drawing the real masterpiece?" Go back over the passage and point out the important details.

 *Watch Out!*

Sometimes fourth graders are drawn to the most interesting or personally relevant details in a passage, and they ignore the details that are most important to the story. For example, your kid might remember that Jade wins a bunch of art supplies and think that this is important because he would like to have a bunch of art supplies. This could filter into his answer for question 4, but this would not be an important-enough detail to focus on for a summary of the whole story.

What to Know...

Writing or identifying good summaries is a difficult skill. Including too many details, including the wrong ones, or missing the most important details are all potential trouble spots, even for strong readers.

Review these skills with your child this way:

- A **detail** is a piece of information in a passage, sometimes given in a word or phrase.
- A **summary** is a retelling of the most important information in a passage or the main points of a story. A summary includes the topic, the major events, the main theme or ideas, or the most important characters. A summary is usually brief.

At school, your child might see a poster like this.

Fourth-Grade Art Contest

- Enter any piece af art you created. This could be a drawing, a mobile, or even a collage.
- Bring your art to Mr. Lopez in room 54 by this Friday.

The winner will get new markers, crayons, and colored pencils. The piece will be placed in the hallway for everyone to see.

Ask your child to summarize the information in this poster.

 *Checking In*

Most kids can pick out details in the poster, such as "fourth grade," "drawing, mobile, or even a collage." But to make a good summary, your child has to figure out what details are most important, such as "Art Contest," dealing with art that "you created."

Your kid can use the important details to summarize the information in the poster:

- Kids can submit any art they created to the fourth-grade art contest to win art supplies and have their art shown in the school.
- Fourth graders need to submit their own drawings, mobiles, or collages to Mr. Lopez if they want to win the art contest.

Children struggle when they recall only less significant details that interest them:

- The winner will get new art supplies.
- Art will be hung in the hallway.

 *Study Right*

Help your child develop a system for keeping track of important details. Some kids like to underline the details in the passage as they read, while others absorb them better by writing these details out on a separate sheet of paper. Your child might create a list or an outline to go with a reading selection. Try to help him or her figure out which approach works best.

Fourth Graders Are...

Your child might be sensitive to negative feedback. Kids this age usually are. Positive words can go a long way—and might have a tremendous impact on his or her mood during these activities. Try to keep your child engaged in these activities with some words of encouragement. A "nice job" or "great work" here and there can really boost your child's interest and confidence.

On Your Way to an "A" Activities

 Type: Arts and Crafts
Materials needed: art supplies, such as markers and crayons, pencils, paper
Number of players: 2 or more

Imagine that your school is holding a talent show. Imagine that your teacher has asked you to make a poster to announce this. What are the important details that you will need to include in the poster? What information will your classmates need to enter the contest? Write these details down on a piece of paper. Then, make a poster. Have fun with the poster and make it as cool as you can—but be sure to include all the important details you wrote down. Share your poster with others. Ask them if you forgot anything important.

 Type: Reading/Writing
Materials needed: a newspaper, pencils, paper
Number of players: 2 or more

Newspaper headlines do a great job summarizing the stories that go with them. Read some articles in the newspaper. Pay close attention to the headlines and titles. How do they summarize the story? Now, ask a friend to cover the headline of a story. Read it together and write your own ideas. Was your title similar to the one the paper used? What information from the story helped you pick out your title?

Has your child breezed through the activities? If so, he or she can work on this Using Your Head activity independently.

Using Your Head

{10} minutes

*Grab a **pencil**!*

As you know from the story on page 46, Jade didn't know what to do when she discovered the scoring error.

Read the paragraph she wrote in her journal that night. As you read, underline important details. Then, answer the questions.

Today, Mr. Kolling told me I won the art contest. I was so happy! I got a red ribbon and a certificate. I also got some art supplies. I got a really neat pen that has glitter ink. Mom and Dad made tacos. I ate two! Then, I discovered something bad. My score was wrong! I didn't really win. I am going to tell Mr. Kolling at school tomorrow. My parents said it is the right thing to do. They also said they are more proud of me for being honest than for winning the contest.

1. The least important detail in Jade's paragraph is that

   A. Mr. Kolling told her she won the art contest

   B. she got a pen filled with glitter ink

   C. she will tell Mr. Kolling about the error at school the next day

2. Jade needs to add one more detail about her day. What detail is the most important one she could include?

   _____

   _____

Answers: 1. B; 2. Mark scored higher than she did in the contest with a 97.

Using Illustrations

In fourth grade, kids sometimes disregard illustrations that go along with the text they're reading. "Those are for little kids," they may say. This makes sense: They've recently graduated from "baby books"—and there's no way they are going back!

The problem, though, is that they might miss some important information. Sometimes, information appears in an illustration—and *not* in the text. If your child enjoys comic books, point out how important the illustrations are. This should drive home the value of illustrations!

Your kid should learn that illustrations and texts often go hand in hand. He or she should learn to value the information in an illustration and use it to reinforce reading comprehension.

First things first: Get a sense of what your kid already knows. Turn the page and tell your kid to Jump Right In!

Here's what you'll need for this lesson:
- *a newspaper or magazine*
- *the comics section of a newspaper*
- *a recipe or a set of directions*
- *art supplies, such as markers or crayons*
- *paper*

Jump Right In!

Make an Icy Treat!

Do you want something cold and delicious? Check with your parents. If they say it's okay, try making these icy treats.

What you'll need:
- Some fruit juice. Be sure to pick your favorite—anything from orange juice to cranberry juice!
- An empty ice cube tray
- Some plastic wrap
- Some toothpicks

A.

Step 1: Pour your favorite juice into an empty ice cube tray.

B.

Step 2: Cover the tray with plastic wrap.

Step 3: Insert one toothpick into each square in the ice cube tray.

C.

Step 4: Place the ice cube tray in the freezer. Let the juice freeze!

Step 5: Take the tray out of the refrigerator. Remove the plastic wrap.

D.

Step 6: Enjoy your mini ice treats!

1. Illustration A shows

    A. what you'll need to complete Step 1

    B. items you can use in place of the real ingredients

    C. everything you'll need to make the treats

    D. the items that cannot be found in a grocery store

2. Illustration B shows

    A. someone completing Step 1 correctly

    B. someone completing Step 2 correctly

    C. someone completing Step 1 incorrectly

    D. someone completing Step 2 incorrectly

3. Why does the recipe include Illustration C?

_____

_____

4. Why does the recipe include Illustration D?

_____

_____

Excellent Job!

 *Checking In*

Ⓐ Answers for page 55:

1. C

2. A

3. An A+ answer: "Illustration C shows what the treats would look like if you've done everything correctly through Step 3."

4. An A+ answer: "Illustration D shows someone enjoying the treats when they are all done. This is what you can expect after you've done everything through Step 6."

Did your child pick the correct answers? If so, ask your child to explain each of the illustrations and the relationship it has to the text.

Did your child get any of the answers wrong? If so, ask, "Why did you choose that answer?" Maybe your child rushed through the question and didn't take time to connect the illustration to the text. You could say, "That's a good try, but how does the illustration relate to the recipe? Let's look at the illustration and the recipe again." For example, for question 2, ask your child to point to Illustration B. Then, ask your child to describe what he sees. Finally, ask your child to read the steps aloud and identify what step is shown in Illustration B.

 *Watch Out!*

If your kid is not taking the information she should from the illustrations in this exercise, you might ask, "Did you think these illustrations would be helpful?" You might point out that Illustration A makes it easy to see everything you need to make the treats. Not only does it reinforce the information written in the recipe, but it's a quick and easy reference to use as you gather your supplies.

What to Know...

Illustrations are very important in many texts, especially with science books and history books. Also, we rely on illustrations every day: bus maps, health pamphlets from the doctor's office, instruction manuals, and so on.

Review this skill with your child this way:

- **Illustrations** often show pictures of topics and events from the passage. Strong readers often use illustrations to make sure they understand what is going on in the passage. They identify details in illustrations and answer questions based on the details in illustrations. Strong readers understand that illustrations and passages go hand in hand and that sometimes illustrations show details not mentioned in the passage.

Your child comes across illustrations every day. You and your child might see a poster like this in your neighborhood.

Bike for sale!

My family and I are moving to the city, and I can't take my bike with me.
It's only five years old and goes super fast. It's light blue, and the back tire is brand new.

Call Juan if you're interested at 555-6868.

Ask your child to identify a detail in the illustration that does *not* appear in the text. Then, ask your child to identify a detail from the text that does *not* appear in the illustration.

Bike for sale!

My family and I are moving to the city, and I can't take my bike with me.
It's only five years old and goes super fast. It's light blue, and the back tire is brand new.

Call Juan if you're interested at 555-6868.

 **Checking In**

Kids should be able to connect the illustration to the text. Your kid may have noticed the following:

- The illustration shows that the bike has a basket on the handlebars and a flag on the back. These details do not appear in the text.
- The text says the bike is only five years old, is blue, and has a new back tire. Your kid wouldn't know this from the illustration.

On Your Way to an "A" Activities

Type: Arts and Crafts
Materials needed: a newspaper or magazine, art supplies, paper
Number of players: 2 or more

Choose an article in a newspaper or magazine. Be sure to pick one that grabs your interest. Then, create an illustration to go with this article. Include at least one detail that appears in the text. Also, include one detail that you make up yourself. This detail should tell readers something new. Decorate the illustration. Have fun with it!

Type: Reading/Writing
Materials needed: comics section of a newspaper, art supplies (markers or crayons are enough), paper
Number of players: 2 or more

Read the comics section of a newspaper. Pay close attention to the relationship between the text and the illustration. Then, create your own comic strip! You might choose to base your comic strip on your favorite one in the newspaper. Be sure to decorate your illustrations with cool colors. For extra fun, do a whole series of comic strips. You can make your own comic book!

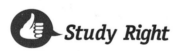 Study Right

It's important for kids to draw a connection between the illustrations and the text. Some illustrations come with captions. These often clarify the relationship between the text and the illustration. If an illustration doesn't have a caption, you might ask your child to provide one as he or she reads. This is a great way for your child to get in the habit of connecting the text and the illustration. It also puts your kid in the driver's seat.

Type: Arts and Crafts
Materials needed: a recipe or a set of directions, art supplies, paper
Number of players: 2

Choose a recipe or a set of directions that does not have any pictures to go with it. You might choose the directions that go with your favorite board game. Create at least four pictures to go with the text. The pictures and the text should go hand in hand. Make sure you decide where your pictures would appear in the text.

Type: Reading/Writing
Materials needed: art supplies, paper, pencils
Number of players: 2 or more

Work with a partner to create two stories with pictures. One player should begin by writing a story. That player should write big and put only a few sentences on each page. At the same time, the second player should draw at least five pictures. Then, swap. The second player should draw illustrations to go with the text that the first person wrote. The first player, meanwhile, should write text to go with the pictures that the second player drew. This will give you two complete stories!

Fourth Graders Are...

Kids this age have no problem learning rules. They even like them! For this reason, they tend to enjoy board games and quickly memorize the rules. You will probably find that the directions and rules that go with board games provide excellent material for activities. Don't be afraid to use things your kid already enjoys to help him strengthen the skills he'll need in the classroom. You might play a board game together and incorporate a learning activity into it.

Using Your Head

{**15** minutes}

*Grab a **pencil**!*

Read the following story. Then, study the illustration on the next page. What details appear in both the illustration *and* the story? Circle these details in the illustration, and underline the details in the text. Then, answer the questions that follow.

Tara's Tenth Birthday

Tara wanted to make something for her birthday party. Her father baked a big white cake, and her mother made a cheese pizza. Her sister made her some funky hats for everyone, and her brother decorated the dining room with streamers.

When she was reading her magazine *Kool Kids,* she found a cool recipe for icy treats. "Can I make these?" she asked her mom.

"Of course!" her mom answered. "I'll help you get everything you need, and then you can take it from there."

"Great!" said Tara. "Can we use apple juice?"

"Sure," her mom answered.

1. What is a detail that appears in the illustration but <u>not</u> the story?

_____

_____

_____

2. Name as many details as possible that appear in the story but <u>not</u> the illustration.

_____

_____

_____

Answers: 1. "Tara invited four friends to her party. There are balloons. Her dad wears glasses." 2. "Tara's mom helped her find everything she needed to make the icy treats. She found the recipe in a magazine."

Genre

Genre is a word that might be unfamiliar to your kid. Kids this age are reading a wide range of texts. They're coming across everything: novels, poems, myths, textbooks, newspaper articles, cookbooks, manuals, and dictionaries. Kids need to be able to distinguish the differences between all these kinds of texts.

But here's the good news: A lot of kids this age enjoy classifying and memorizing things. In school, your kid might be asked to memorize the multiplication table, the state capitals, or even the Gettysburg Address. Don't be surprised if he or she enjoys this!

However, classifying a piece of literature can be a little tricky. Your kid will need to analyze it. This skill doesn't come overnight—but it can be developed and sharpened as your child reads more and more.

First things first: Get a sense of what your kid already knows. Turn the page and tell your kid to Jump Right In!

Here's what you'll need for this lesson:
- art supplies, such as crayons, markers, and anything else you have
- a collection of books
- paper
- pencils

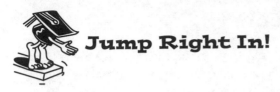

Jump Right In!

Luci Tapahonso

Luci Tapahonso is a well-known Navajo writer. She grew up in Shiprock, New Mexico. She was one of 11 children! She studied English at the University of New Mexico. Her work includes a book called *Blue Horses Rush In.* She now lives in Tucson, Arizona, and teaches at the University of Arizona.

1. This is an example of

    A. a poem

    B. a biography

    C. a short story

    D. a fable

My Pet Hamster Is a Superstar

My hamster is a ham.
He likes to roll on his back,
Then huddle in his hamster can,
And peek out through the crack.

2. This is an example of

    A. an autobiography

    B. a newspaper article

    C. a myth

    D. a poem

The Grasshoppers

A group of grasshoppers lived deep in a forest. They all got along well, but one of the grasshoppers worried. He thought the other grasshoppers didn't like him. He worried so much that he started saying bad things about the other grasshoppers. These things weren't true, but the grasshopper wanted to make everyone else look bad. He thought this would make him look good. Instead, the opposite happened. No one trusted him anymore.

3. Do you think this story is fiction or nonfiction? Explain your answer. In what kind of book would this story appear?

_____

_____

Excellent Job!

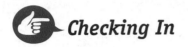

Checking In

Ⓐ Answers for pages 64 and 65:

    1. B

    2. D

    3. An A+ answer: "This story is a fable. It is fiction. The events never happened. They are all imaginary."

Did your child pick the correct answers? If so, ask your child to explain his or her choices. You might ask, "How did you know that this was a biography?" or "How could you tell this was a poem?" Have your kid explain the differences between the passages.

Did your child get any of the answers wrong? If so, explain that "Luci Tapahonso" is a biography, that "My Pet Hamster Is a Superstar" is a poem, and that "The Grasshoppers" is fiction. Then, ask, "What is the difference between a biography and a poem?" Your child might not know what a biography is or how to identify a poem. To help her out, you could say, "A biography tells about a person's life and it's a true story" or "A poem often rhymes and isn't written in paragraphs."

Watch Out!

A lot of the words in this lesson might be new to your kid. Words like *myth* and *fable* might be unfamiliar to your kid. Make sure he or she understands what these two words mean. You might say, "A fable is a story that teaches a lesson. The characters are usually animals." For a myth, you might say, "In a myth, the story takes place a long, long time ago. It often includes ancient peoples and their heroes."

What to Know...

As your child becomes a stronger and stronger reader, he or she will start discerning the differences in genre. Your child might already be noticing what traits make up different genres. This skill will come in very handy for your kid's future writing endeavors as well as for all of the reading he or she does in the future.

Review these skills with your child this way:

- A **genre** is a particular type of literary work. **Novels, short stories, plays, poetry,** myths, newspapers, reference books, and **essays** are some genres.
- **Fiction** tells a made-up story. Fiction tells a story with imagined characters and events. Stories, plays, and fairy tales are examples of fiction. **Novels, short stories, plays, poetry,** and **essays** are some genres of literature.
- **Nonfiction** tells only facts and true information. Textbooks are examples of nonfiction.

Your child might encounter a list of books like this:

- *Landing on My Feet: A Diary of Dreams* by Kerri Strug
- *To Kill a Mockingbird* by Harper Lee
- *The Diary of Anne Frank* by Anne Frank
- *What If You Met a Pirate?* by Jan Adkins
- *Mr. Popper's Penguins* by Richard Atwater
- *Henry Huggins* by Beverly Cleary
- *How Ben Franklin Stole the Lightning* by Rosalyn Schanzer

· · · · · · · · · · · · · · · ·

Ask your child to identify each of these books as either fiction or nonfiction.

 *Checking In*

The title of a book can sometimes help kids to distinguish fiction from nonfiction.

- The nonfiction books are *Landing on My Feet: A Diary of Dreams, The Diary of Anne Frank,* and *How Ben Franklin Stole the Lightning.*
- The fiction books are *To Kill a Mockingbird, What If You Met a Pirate?, Mr. Popper's Penguins,* and *Henry Huggins.*

On Your Way to an "A" Activities

{ 45 minutes } Type: Game/Competitive
Materials needed: none
Number of players: 2 or more

Go on a scavenger hunt! Make a list of different types of writing. Your list might include a poem, a myth, a fable, an encyclopedia entry, an autobiography, a recipe, a play, a newspaper article, a novel, or a short story. Then, try to find one example of each genre in 30 minutes. Make sure that you correctly identify and keep track of each example. You can play this game at home, or you can go to the library. Whoever collects the most examples wins!

{ 15 minutes } Type: Active
Materials needed: a collection of books
Number of players: 2 or more

Have one player gather a big stack of books. These books should all be very different. That player should read the first few sentences from each book out loud, one book at a time. If the book is fiction, the listener should clap three times. If it's nonfiction, the listener should snap his or her fingers three times. Separate the books that the listener identified correctly and incorrectly. The listener should take a closer look at the ones he or she got wrong.

Fourth Graders Are...

Kids this age often like order. Even though their bedrooms might be a mess, they like their classrooms clean and organized. For this reason, they might enjoy classifying different types of writing. Classifying things helps us put the world around us in order, and this lesson will appeal to your kid's wish to create order.

Type: Reading/Writing
Materials needed: art supplies, paper, pencils
Number of players: 2

Tackle a genre a day! Start with a list of different genres: novels, short stories, plays, poems, myths, fables, textbooks, newspapers, magazine articles, autobiographies, encyclopedias, reference books (such as a dictionary or thesaurus), cookbooks, and manuals. Each day, start with a clean sheet of paper. At the top, write a genre and then define it. List three examples of books that belong in that genre. Then, write your own. You might write a paragraph of a story you've made up, or a few lines of a poem. Keep all of your sheets together. When you are done, you have your very own genre book! Make a cool cover for it. Be sure to refer to it if you're ever confused.

Study Right

Some kids have trouble with the difference between fiction and nonfiction. They might know that one involves imaginary people, but they can't remember which one. To help your kid keep the distinction clear, you might have your child create two posters, one for fiction and one for nonfiction. The poster for fiction should have the important characteristics of fiction on it, and the one for nonfiction should have the important characteristics of nonfiction. Hang these where your kid will see them.

Has your child breezed through the activities? If so, he or she can work on this Using Your Head activity independently.

Using Your Head

{ **60** minutes }

*Grab some **paper**, a **pencil**, and some **art supplies**!*

Think of someone you admire. You might choose someone famous that you see on TV or someone at school you think is cool. Then, write about this person in several different ways.

You should try to write all of the following:

- A poem about that person
- A paragraph that tells an imaginary story involving that person (Pretend that this paragraph will appear in a novel.)
- A scene from a play that includes that person
- An encyclopedia entry that describes that person's life
- A newspaper article that tells about an exciting event involving that person

Feel free to add illustrations to your texts. Be creative and have fun! When you are done, put all of your writings together. You have your very own book.

If you chose someone you know, feel free to share your creation with that person.

Main Idea

The difference between the main idea of a text and a summary of it is a subtle one, but it's important that your kid understand. A summary is a shortened version of a text. It gives the gist of the text. It might be a few sentences and the key details, and it sometimes contains the main idea. A main idea, however, is the main point that the author wants to get across. It is best conveyed in one sentence.

Fourth graders are full of ideas and explanations. This can get them into trouble when they're trying to come up with the main idea of a passage. They may rely on their imaginations—and ignore important details.

First things first: Get a sense of what your kid already knows. Turn the page and tell your kid to Jump Right In!

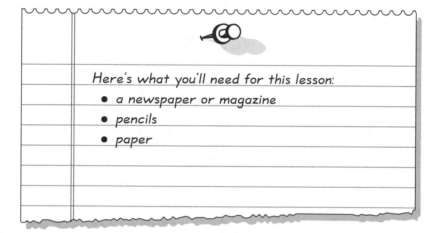

Here's what you'll need for this lesson:
- a newspaper or magazine
- pencils
- paper

 **Jump Right In!**

Kiki and Cora's Decision

Kiki and Cora had always dreamed of forming an all-girl singing group. They loved Destiny's Child, listened to the Supremes all day, and couldn't get enough of En Vogue. "Now it's our turn," said Kiki. "All we need is a third girl."

They asked twelve girls to come and sing for them. They served pink lemonade in Cora's attic bedroom and listened as each one sang a sample song. Marvina sang *Tootie Fruitie,* Diana sang *Happy Birthday,* and Mary made up a song on the spot.

Once everyone left, Kiki and Cora sat down to decide who to pick.

"They're all so good," Kiki said.

"But we can only choose one," answered Cora. "So let's narrow it down to three." The two girls made a list.

First, there was Phoebe. She could hit the highest notes in any song. "We need someone like her for those power ballads," said Kiki, biting into a cookie.

"What are power ballads?" Cora asked. Kiki wasn't sure. "Who else is there?" Cora asked.

"There's Flora," said Kiki. "She's super tall, so she'll make us look like two ants."

"But she has a cool voice," said Cora, "and she plays the piano."

"You're right," said Kiki. "But who else?"

"Fluff!" answered Cora. Fluff seemed like a star, mostly because of her name (her real name was Griselda, but only her parents called her that).

"She told me she wants to sell one million records before she turns 15," said Kiki.

Cora looked confused. "I don't know if I have time to sell one million records," she said. "I have soccer practice after school— and math is really hard this year."

The two girls couldn't decide. Cora sighed. Kiki shrugged. "I know!" said Kiki. "Let's decide after we listen to En Vogue."

1. What is the main idea of the first paragraph?

   A. Kiki and Cora want to be famous.

   B. Kiki and Cora listen to Destiny's Child all the time.

   C. Kiki and Cora want to form a singing group like the ones they listen to.

   D. Kiki and Cora have a tough decision to make about their third member.

2. What is the main idea of the second paragraph?

   A. Cora's attic is the perfect place for the girls to sing.

   B. Kiki and Cora listen to twelve girls in their search for a singer.

   C. Mary makes up a song on her own and sings it for the girls.

   D. Kiki and Cora think all of the girls are good.

3. What is the main idea of the whole passage?

   _____

   _____

Excellent Job!

 *Checking In*

❹Answers for page 73:

    1. C

    2. B

    3. An A+ answer: "Kiki and Cora find that trying out other singers for their all-girl singing group is more work than they planned on."

Did your child get the correct answers? If so, have your child explain her understanding of the main idea of the passage and how she came to it.

Did your child get any of the answers wrong? If so, make sure your child focused on the paragraph that the question was asking about. You might ask, "Tell me what that paragraph is about in one sentence." If this sentence doesn't seem to be the main idea of the paragraph, go back over it together. Have your kid recount what happens and then write out a single sentence that captures the point of the paragraph. For example, with question 1, your kid may have chosen the first answer because this seems like an important point. But the main idea of that paragraph isn't that these girls share a bunch of dreams; it's one particular dream. Stating the main idea requires that your kid do something more with the details from a passage than just recount them.

 *Watch Out!*

Determining the main idea can be a frustrating skill for fourth graders to learn. They probably want a clear rule to follow or memorize, but finding the main idea can be tricky. Sometimes it's in the first sentence, and sometimes it's in the last sentence. Sometimes, it's not even stated outright. You need to teach your kid to be careful when reading for the main idea. After she is done reading, you could say, "In *one* sentence, tell me what you just read." This should help her to distill the main idea.

What to Know...

Kids might run into trouble identifying the main idea of a text. They might not know which details support the main idea—and which are included simply to make the text more interesting.

Review these skills with your child this way:

- A **main idea** is a statement of what a passage is mostly about. Often, an author states the main idea in the first or last sentences of the passage. However, an author may state the main idea anywhere in the passage. An author also may choose not to state the main idea directly, in which case the reader has to infer the main idea of the passage.

- **Details** are bits of information in a passage, sometimes given in a word or a phrase.

- Regarding a main idea, a **supporting detail** is a detail from the passage that supports the main idea. Sometimes, there are details in a passage that contradict the main idea.

Your child might come across a paragraph like this in his or her reading:

> No one ever went inside the old Pierce house on the corner. Ivy covered its walls, and wooden boards hid its windows. The stairs leading up to it were nice, though. Stray cats lived under the porch, and a dark raven often stood on its roof. White paint peeled off the outside walls. Everyone was scared of the house.

Ask your child to tell you the main idea of the paragraph. You might ask, "Did one sentence help you determine the main idea? If so, which one?" Ask your child to identify a supporting detail. Finally, ask your child to identify one detail that does *not* support the main idea.

 *Checking In*

Your kid should be able to determine the main idea and supporting details:

- The main idea should be something like this: "The old Pierce house was empty and falling apart" or "The Pierce house was really spooky."

- The first and last sentences are very helpful in determining the main idea.

- The paragraph includes many supporting details, such as wooden boards hiding its windows and stray cats living under its porch.

- The only detail that doesn't support the main idea is that the stairs were nice.

On Your Way to an "A" Activities

45 minutes

Type: Speaking/Listening
Materials needed: none
Number of players: 2 or more

Think about a movie that you're familiar with and come up with a single main-idea statement about this movie. Then, watch part of the movie and keep a list of details in one column that support the main idea. In another column, make a list of details that do not support the main idea. Finally, compare lists with the other players. See who came up with the best main idea and supporting details. You might have to go over each other's lists to make sure that the details actually support the main ideas you've come up with.

15 minutes

Type: Reading/Writing
Materials needed: pencil and paper
Number of players: 2 or more

Think of a statement you believe to be true. Write it at the top of a piece of paper. This might be something like, "The best pet to have is a dog" or "Television is boring." Then, come up with a list of details to support this idea. Finally, think of some details that do *not* support this idea.

Type: Reading/Writing

Materials needed: newspaper or magazine, paper, pencils

Number of players: 2 or more

Read an article in a newspaper or magazine. Write down the main idea of each paragraph. Then, write down the main idea of the entire article. Give the article a new title. Make sure that your title reflects the main idea!

 *Study Right*

You might encourage your kid to write down main ideas as he or she reads. After each paragraph, your kid might jot down a note in the margins or on a separate piece of paper that describes the main idea in that paragraph or section. If your kid gets stuck, ask him or her to think, "In one sentence, what does all of this say?" Determining the main idea will increase your child's reading comprehension, and taking notes while reading is a good habit for your child to develop early.

Fourth Graders Are...

Fourth graders work well in teams. They enjoy sharing their knowledge with other kids, so group projects really appeal to them. If you find that your child learns well with others, encourage her to work in groups. Have her friends join in with these activities.

Using Your Head

[30 minutes]

Grab a **pencil** and some **paper**!

Cora and Kiki chose Flora as the third girl for their new all-girl singing group.

They wrote, "Flora is the best choice for our singing group" at the top of their notes. Their notes appear below. Circle the details that support this idea. Draw a line through the details that do not.

- Plays piano
- Interesting voice
- Voice blends well with ours
- Is a Capricorn
- Gets along well with us
- Didn't finish her pink lemonade
- Works really hard
- Loves music
- Has two brothers
- Can sing high notes

Now, suppose you were rooting for Fluff. You might say, "Fluff is the best choice for Cora and Kiki's singing group." Write a paragraph using this statement as your main idea. Include at least three details to support your main idea. You can make up these details, but they must support your main idea. Have fun with it!

Inferences and Conclusions

I**f you saw a car with a dented door, you might say, "I bet that car was in an accident." However, your child might say something wildly imaginative, something like, "I bet that a giant lizard stomped on that car door!" As a parent, you probably love those moments. But when it comes to reading skills, the imaginative and creative side of a child can get in the way of what he or she has been asked to do.

With schoolwork, kids need to know that they have to stick to the details that are in front of them. To correctly answer conclusion or inference questions, your child needs to use the details within the passage. If there's no giant lizard in the passage, then there's no chance a giant lizard dented the door, and there should be no giant lizard in the correct answer.

First things first: Get a sense of what your kid already knows. Turn the page and tell your kid to Jump Right In!

Here's what you'll need for this lesson:
- a photo or music
- a newspaper with photos or access to an online news Web site with photos
- a bag
- a blindfold
- crayons
- instruction manuals, directions, cookbooks, etc.
- paper and pencils

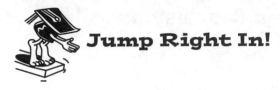
Jump Right In!

Tessa and the Treasure

Tessa poked her head into her grandmother's attic. She gasped. She couldn't believe all of the stuff piled up. She and her family were helping her grandmother clean her house.

She was glad she had volunteered to be the one to clean the attic. "Who knows what I might find up here?" she said to herself. "I might find a hidden treasure!" She opened the first box.

"Certainly no treasure here," she thought. The box was full of gray socks and old rags. Another box was full of old telephone bills. No one would want to keep this stuff. So, these boxes could go to the curb. She pushed them into a pile near the stairs.

She found several boxes of old clothing that they could give to the homeless shelter. So, she pushed these boxes into a second pile. Still no treasure pile. Tessa began to worry.

It was after lunch that Tessa made her discovery. She shoved a box into the curb pile without looking into it, but then she peered inside. "Oh my goodness!" she said. "These are magazines Grandma must have saved from her childhood!" Each magazine was carefully sealed in a plastic bag. The magazines were more than 60 years old, but they looked brand new. She called her parents. Together they also found old record albums that were still in their original wrappings.

"These are probably very valuable because they are so well cared for," said Tessa's father. "Your grandmother knew these things were important enough to keep, so I think we should do the same. I'll put them in our attic."

"Maybe someday I can give them to my grandchildren," said Tessa. "They will be even more valuable then."

"That's a good idea, Tessa," said her mother. "Maybe that's why Grandma put them in the attic in the first place!"

1. Grandma put the magazines and albums in the attic years ago so that she could
   A. look at them again when she was 60 years old
   B. listen to the records whenever she wanted
   C. sell them and make a lot of money
   D. save them for her grandchildren

2. Tessa was most likely worried that
   A. she would take a long time to clean the attic
   B. she wouldn't find any hidden treasures in the attic
   C. her grandmother needed to keep the telephone bills
   D. all the boxes would contain socks and rags

3. Why did Grandma seal each magazine in a plastic bag?

   _____

   _____

4. What details support your answer to question 3?

   _____

   _____

Excellent Job!

 *Checking In*

AAnswers for page 81:

    1. D

    2. B

    3. An A+ answer: "Grandma sealed each magazine to keep them looking brand new and to make sure they'd be worth money."

    4. An A+ answer: "The passage says that Grandma saved them since her childhood, that they looked brand new, and that they are worth money because they are so well cared for."

Did your child get the correct answers? If so, tell your child to underline the details that he or she used. Have her explain how these details helped her answer the questions.

Did your child get any of the answers wrong? If so, ask, "Why did you pick that answer?" Maybe your child used information from his or her personal experience instead of using only information from the passage. For example, for question 2, your kid may have chosen A as his answer because he knows that cleaning an attic takes a while. You could say, "That's an interesting idea, and it's true that it does take some time to clean the attic, but is that what Tessa's concerned about? Look at the passage again."

 *Watch Out!*

Sometimes fourth graders insert their own experiences into stories. Maybe your child's chore is to put twist-ties on the garbage bags so the garbage doesn't fall out, and so your child wrote, "Her Grandma sealed the magazines in plastic bags so they wouldn't fall out with the garbage" for question 3. When you see your kid losing focus on the details in the story, guide him or her back. Ask your kid to point out the details in the story they can use to answer the question.

What to Know...

It's easy to get inferences and conclusions confused. The most important thing your child needs to know is that inferences and conclusions are both ideas or thoughts based on facts or observations.

Review these skills with your child this way:

- An **inference** or a **conclusion** is an idea or thought based on details.
- **Details** are facts and observations. The details in a passage are bits of information, sometimes given in a word or phrase.
- When teachers ask for an inference or conclusion about a passage, it must be based on the details in the passage.

Your child sees details and makes inferences and conclusions every day. You and your child might see a poster like this in your neighborhood.

- Black spots
- Last seen Monday near the park
- Call Ariella if you find him

 *Checking In*

Most kids can use the details to make inferences or conclusions:

- The dog is lost.
- Ariella is probably the dog's owner.
- Ariella and the dog were near the park when the dog was lost.

Children struggle when they make assumptions or leap to conclusions or inferences **not** supported by these details:

- The dog doesn't like Ariella.
- The dog was lost on Sunday.
- The dog lives in the park.

· · · · · · · · · · · · · · · · ·

Ask your child to tell you a story based on the poster, about who may have put up the poster and why.

On Your Way to an "A" Activities

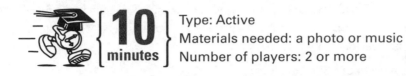

Type: Active
Materials needed: a photo or music
Number of players: 2 or more

Look at a photo or listen to music. Start with an obvious detail such as, "I am in the photo" or "The lead singer in the song is a woman." Then, take turns with your partner finding more and more difficult-to-observe details, such as, "There is a bird on the tree in the background of the photo" or "I hear a flute playing softly in the background of the song." Challenge yourselves to identify more and more details.

Type: Game/Competitive
Materials needed: a newspaper with photos, a pencil, and some paper
Number of players: 2

Play "News Investigator." Find a news article with a photo. Look at the photo with your partner. Each player should write down a list of things that the news article could be about, based on the photo. Then, read the news article and give yourself a point for each correct conclusion and inference on your list. Whoever has the most points wins.

Fourth Graders Are...

Your child might feel pretty strongly about issues of fairness. Competitions and counting points can be a big deal for fourth graders. So, with any "Game/Competitive" activity, be very clear about the rules and point system. You could also avoid counting points and just have fun with these activities!

Type: Reading/Writing
Materials needed: a bag, a blindfold, instruction manuals, directions, guides, cookbooks, and such
Number of players: 2

Find several different kinds of books that include directions (cookbooks, owner's manuals, etc.). Put them into a bag. Put on the blindfold and pick out a book. Your partner should read a few sentences out loud. Make an inference about the type of book you picked. If you are correct, then switch and take turns. Your partner should keep reading until you guess correctly.

Type: Game/Competitive
Materials needed: paper and pencils
Number of players: 2 or more

Play the game "Charades." Think of a person you all know. Write the person's name on a piece of paper and list details that would show who the person is. Then, "perform" those details, acting like the person—no talking! The other players have to guess who the person is. Once they have guessed correctly, switch roles.

 *Study Right*

Taking clear notes can help children remember the details from a passage. If you have to remember details about something—like movie times, grocery lists, etc.—demonstrate this skill by making a neat list. Label the list, and if you don't need something, draw a line through it. Your child should draw a line through details that don't support a conclusion and through wrong answer choices. Explain how drawing a line means you can still read those details—so it will be easier for you to read them again if you need to.

Has your child breezed through the activities? If so, he or she can work on this Using Your Head activity independently.

Using Your Head

{10 minutes}

*Grab some **crayons**!*

Tessa's grandmother said that she also saved old, valuable toys. Draw a line through any clues in the attic that don't lead to toys. Then, circle the clues that point to the treasured toys, and color any toys you spot.

1. Where should Tessa definitely look for the toys?

_____

Answer: Tessa should definitely look in the ties box and the suits closet.

Cracking the Fourth Grade

Plot, Setting, and Characters

Fourth graders might have a hard time with words such as *plot, setting,* and *characters*. These words might sound like technical terms that their reading teacher asks them about. What your kid might not realize is that every story he or she reads includes these elements.

You can encourage your kid to think of himself as a character and of life as a story. Wherever your kid is—that's the setting. The people he meets and spends time with—those are other characters in the story. And everything that happens in a day? That's the plot!

You may remember how you were taught to think about reading using these questions: who, what, when, where, how, and why. By thinking about plot, setting, and characters, your kid is thinking about these questions. Setting is where and when. Characters are who and usually why. And plot is what and how. She will be reading a lot in fourth grade, and thinking about plot, setting, and characters will give her a way to keep the details straight.

First things first: Get a sense of what your kid already knows. Turn the page and tell your kid to Jump Right In!

Here's what you'll need for this lesson:
- art supplies, such as crayons, markers, glitter, sparkles, pipe cleaners, and felt
- two short stories
- pencils
- paper

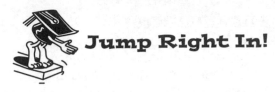 **Jump Right In!**

Paz and the Sunflower

Every morning on his way to school, Paz passed the museum. He waved to Ms. Sato, who took tickets from visitors. He looked at the lawn in front of the building.

One spring morning, he noticed something interesting as he stood over a dirt patch where the cement sidewalk was broken. A few green leaves peeked up from the ground. It was a new sunflower.

At school that day, he told his teacher, Mr. Brown, about his discovery. "I wonder how that plant got there?" Paz asked.

"Maybe a bird dropped a seed from its mouth, or the wind blew the seed there," Mr. Brown explained. "If a seed finds the right soil and gets enough water, it will grow."

Paz watched the plant grow a little more every day. "It's my little friend," he thought. The spring rains kept the plant strong and healthy.

"You're happy," Paz said to it one afternoon. The plant had grown a lovely yellow flower. It looked like the sun, and the stem was taller than Paz!

Then one day, Paz passed the plant and noticed it seemed sad. Its leaves were droopy. "You don't look so good," Paz said.

Ms. Sato, who was passing by, heard him. "It needs water, Paz," she said. "It's too far from the museum's sprinklers and the rains have stopped." She looked worried as she got in her car and drove away.

That evening at home, Paz thought about the sunflower. At dinner, he told his parents all about it. His father had an idea. "Why don't you water it, Paz?" he asked. "You pass by it every day."

Paz thought about this. His father was right! He would look in his parents' gardening book after dinner and find out exactly how much water it would need, and he would make sure he gave that exact amount to the plant.

"You'll be fine, my friend," Paz whispered to himself. Then, he took a sip of his water.

1. When Ms. Sato tells Paz that the sunflower needs water, they are

   A. at Paz's school

   B. at Paz's home

   C. near the library

   D. in front of the museum

2. At first, the sunflower was strong and healthy because

   A. the museum's sprinklers watered it every day

   B. Ms. Sato took care of it

   C. the spring rains gave it enough water

   D. Mr. Brown watered it every morning

3. How would you describe Paz?

   _____

   _____

   _____

Excellent Job!

 *Checking In*

Answers for page 89:

1. D

2. C

3. An A+ answer: "Paz is very thoughtful. He wants to take care of the sunflower that is growing near the museum. He wants to make sure that it is okay."

Did your child pick the correct answers? If so, ask your child to describe other characters in the story, such as Ms. Sato, Mr. Brown, Paz's mother and father, and the sunflower (explain that plants and animals can be characters too).

Did your child get any of the answers wrong? Maybe your child did not rely on information in the passage. For example, in question 2, your kid may have thought that Ms. Sato took care of the sunflower because she tells Paz what the plant needs. You could say, "That's a good try, but what information in the passage led you to that answer?" Go back over that passage and point out that the plant is lacking water because the rains have stopped. Then, look the passage over together while identifying the characters and the setting.

 *Watch Out!*

Sometimes kids struggle with questions about characters. Your kid might think too broadly and imagine all the different ways that Paz could have responded to the situation with the sunflower, rather than focusing only on the text. Remind him to base his answers on the passage. Your kid also might come up with only a basic description of Paz, such as "He is a boy." If so, ask your kid to come up with three descriptions of Paz based on the passage.

What to Know...

The plot, setting, and characters in a story often change, making it difficult for kids to keep them straight. Sometimes these elements aren't even stated outright. In that case, your kid needs to look for clues to identify them. The most important thing is that she pay attention to any details that reveal these elements as she reads.

Review these skills with your child this way:

- The **plot** is the series of events related in a fictional story.

- The **setting** is the time and place in which the events in a fictional story take place.

- **Characters** are the people whose actions, ideas, thoughts, and feelings a passage tells us about. Characters aren't always human. Sometimes animals, plants, or parts of the setting may be characters in a passage. Authors reveal character through details about the character, including what the character says and how the character behaves.

Your child might come across the following paragraph in a book:

> Daphne found a shady spot in a park near her home. She sat on the ground and placed her writing pad and pen on the grass. Her bright orange skirt fanned out over her ankles. She wanted to write a poem that afternoon. "What should I write?" she asked herself. "Maybe I'll write about that tree over there." She studied the tree for a long time and made some notes.

 *Checking In*

· · · · · · · · · · · · · · ·
Ask your child to identify the plot, setting, and characters in the paragraph.

Your kid should be able to identify the plot, setting, and characters from the paragraph.

- The plot can be summarized as follows: In the paragraph, Daphne finds a spot in a park to write a poem.

- The story takes place in a park during the afternoon.

- Daphne is a character in the paragraph.

On Your Way to an "A" Activities

15 { minutes }

Type: Active
Materials needed: a short story
Number of players: 2 or more

One player should read, and the others should listen carefully. Whenever the story offers a clue about the setting, the listeners should clap three times. For example, if the story says, "He went to the refrigerator" or "It was early in the morning," the listeners should clap. This tells you that the character is in the kitchen. Each time someone claps, the reader should pause so the group can make sure that player identified a clue about the setting. When you are done, you can read the story again or read a new story, and this time everyone can clap when you read a clue about a character.

30 { minutes }

Type: Arts and Crafts
Materials needed: art supplies, such as crayons, markers, glitter, sparkles, pipe cleaners, felt, paper
Number of players: 2 or more

Think of a book you read recently. Who was your favorite character? How would you describe this character? Is this person greedy or kind? Smart or silly? Make sure that you base your description on details from the story. Now, create a picture of this person. Your picture should show what kind of person this character is. Hang your picture on your wall!

Fourth Graders Are...

Kids this age can take things very seriously. Their senses of humor might not always shine through. Encourage them to enjoy themselves. If your kid seems reluctant or shy, join in. Show your kid that even adults can have fun with art projects!

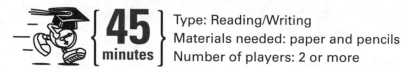

Type: Reading/Writing
Materials needed: paper and pencils
Number of players: 2 or more

Write down two characters and two settings. Remember to include a time and a place for each of your settings. Then, come up with one word to describe each character. This means your list might be something like, "Jack is kind, Laura is smart, a classroom at noon, and a library after school." Then, switch lists with a partner. Write a story using the characters and settings you are given. Make sure your story has a plot. Also, make sure you include details that show that the character fits his or her description. For example, if you were given Jack, you might show that he is kind by having him save a stray dog he found outside the library after school. When you're done, read your stories out loud. For extra fun, create an illustration to go with your story.

 *Study Right*

Sometimes it can be hard to keep track of the plot, setting, and characters in stories with a lot of twists and turns. You might suggest that your kid note these elements in the margins, or keep a list on a separate sheet of paper.

Has your child breezed through the activities? If so, he or she can work on this Using Your Head activity independently.

Using Your Head

{60} minutes

*Grab a **pencil** and some **paper**!*

Go back to the story "Paz and the Sunflower." Make a list of all the characters in the story. Write down at least one word to describe each character. Make sure you use details from the story to come up with these words. Then, list all the settings (times and places) in the story.

After you have finished your list, use it to write what could happen next in the story. Write one paragraph that continues the story where the author left off.

You can continue the story with what happens the next day or even what happens later that evening. It's up to you. In your paragraph, include at least two characters from the story. Have your paragraph take place in a setting that has already appeared in the story. Also, include a detail that shows each character's personality. For example, if you said that Mr. Brown is smart, then include a detail that supports this.

Sequence

Kids in fourth grade often have a great deal of structure in their lives. They follow lists that tell them what to do, when to do it, and how to do it. Your kid's day can be very ordered: First there's attendance, which leads to reading, then math, then recess, then spelling, then lunch, etc. Her days probably unfold pretty similarly.

Even though there's all of this sequencing in their lives, the sequence of events in a text can be pretty tough for kids to figure out. The order of events may not always be immediately clear, especially if a character in a story is describing a memory or something he or she plans to do in the future. It takes patience and careful attention to determine the sequence of events in a passage.

First things first: Get a sense of what your kid already knows. Turn the page and tell your kid to Jump Right In!

Here's what you'll need for this lesson:
- art supplies, such as markers, crayons, felt, glitter, sparkles, glue, fabric, and paper
- a pencil
- a recipe (and the items that the recipe calls for) feel free to use the recipe in Lesson 6, "Make an Icy Treat!"

Jump Right In!

Keisha's Science Journal

"Mom! Mom!" yelled Keisha, running into the living room. "Where is it?"

Keisha's mom put down her knitting. "Where is what, Keisha? Please calm down. I can't help you if you're yelling."

"I'm sorry, Mom," said Keisha. Keisha took a deep breath, then continued, "I can't find my science journal."

"Oh my!" said Keisha's mom.

Keisha treasured her journal. She wrote all of her scientific discoveries in this notebook. She described the hummingbirds in the backyard and took careful notes on all of the plants in the house. It was her most prized possession.

"Sit down," Keisha's mom said. "Think carefully. When did you last see it?"

Keisha thought hard. "I wrote in it yesterday. After school, I noticed some ants in the front yard, so I went out to study them. Later on, while I was helping you with dinner, I noticed that the water in the ice cube tray expanded when the water in it froze, and I know I wrote about that."

Keisha's mom smiled. "I saw you write that in your journal at the table in the kitchen, so you had your journal then."

"That's true," said Keisha. "Then, after dinner, I was watching the moths by the light on the back porch. I wrote in it then too."

Keisha looked worried. "But I already checked the back porch!"

"Well, after you went to bed, your father mentioned that it was going to rain during the night. Maybe he saw your journal on the back porch and was worried that it would get wet," said Keisha's mom. "Did you look on the table by the back door?"

Keisha's face lit up. She bolted to the table. "Found it, Mom!" she yelled.

1. In the story, which of these happened *first*?

    A. Keisha helped her mother with dinner.

    B. Keisha studied ants in the front yard.

    C. Keisha studied moths on the back porch.

    D. Keisha's father said it was going to rain.

2. In the story, which of these happened *last*?

    A. Keisha burst into the living room, calling for her mother.

    B. Keisha's mom remembered something Keisha's father said the night before.

    C. Keisha raced to the table by the back door.

    D. Keisha's mom put down her knitting.

3. What is one thing Keisha did *before* helping her mother prepare dinner?

    _____

    _____

4. In this story, do you learn about the events in the same order in which they actually took place? Explain your answer.

    _____

    _____

Excellent Job!

 *Checking In*

Answers for page 97:

1. B

2. C

3. An A+ answer: "Before helping her mother with dinner, Keisha studied some ants in the front yard."

4. An A+ answer: "No, we learn about the events in a different order. Keisha tells us what she did the day before. This means that events that happened the day before are being told to us *after* the day in which the story actually takes place."

Did your child pick the correct answers? If so, ask her to show you where each of the answer choices appears in the passage. She could underline these events in the passage and then number them to show the order in which they happened.

Did your child get any of the answers wrong? Maybe he rushed through these questions. He needs to take his time to answer correctly. You could say, "That's definitely something that happens, but now lets look at the passage together to see the order of events." Then, go over the passage with him and number the events in the order they happened.

 *Watch Out!*

Determining the order in a reading text asks kids to make sense of things that may not happen in linear time. While fourth graders often enjoy structured lists and order, this is a bit more of a challenge for them. You might point out the order that they have in their lives. You could say, "You always brush your teeth, say good night, and then go to bed."

What to Know...

Some kids may run into trouble trying to keep the order of events clear. They might forget what happened first, especially if the events in a passage are not presented in chronological order.

Review these skills with your child this way:

- **Sequence** is the order of ideas and events in a passage. The sequence in which events are presented in a passage may not be the same as the order in which the events described actually took place.
- Children can describe sequence using the words *before* and *after*.

Your kid has probably played hide-and-seek. Look at these out-of-order game rules.

How to Play Hide-and-Seek

- As the seeker counts, everyone else should hide.
- Pick one person to be the seeker.
- Gather all of your players together.
- The seeker should search for the other players.
- The seeker should count to 100.
- Whomever the seeker finds becomes the new seeker, and the game repeats.

 *Checking In*

Ask your child to put these instructions in order.

Your kid should be able to determine the correct order of events:

- Gather all of your players together.
- Pick one person to be the seeker.
- The seeker should count to 100.
- As the seeker counts, everyone else should hide.
- The seeker should search for the other players.
- Whomever the seeker finds becomes the new seeker, and the game repeats.

On Your Way to an "A" Activities

[10 minutes] Type: Speaking/Listening
Materials needed: none
Number of players: 2 or more

Think of a game you like to play. It might be a board game or a game with cards, or even something like Freeze Tag. Then, tell the others how to play the game. Make sure you explain the directions in the correct order. You might use words such as *first, second, then,* and *last.* When you're done, ask the others if you missed anything, and have them repeat back the sequence the players are supposed to follow.

[30 minutes] Type: Arts and Crafts
Materials needed: art supplies, such as markers, crayons, felt, glitter, sparkles, glue, fabric, paper
Number of players: 2 or more

One player should be the artist, one player should be the recorder, and the other players should decide what the artist does. The artist should begin with a blank sheet of paper. The others should give directions to the artist, and the recorder should write down each direction in order. These might be, "Draw a big house with a chimney." After the artist completes each thing, the others should give more directions. "Add some flowers to the front yard and then some clouds to the sky." The artist must draw only what he or she is told to draw. When the picture is done, the recorder should quiz the other players to see if they remember the sequence of the drawing.

Type: Game/Competitive
Materials needed: none
Number of players: 2 or more

Play "In My Suitcase I Packed…." Choose one player to start. This player should think of an object and then say, "In my suitcase, I packed…" and finish the sentence with the object. The next player should repeat this and then add another object. The next player should repeat the first two objects and then add another object. Everyone needs to repeat the objects in the same order in which they were said. The first player to forget an object—or the correct order in which they were said—loses. But that person gets to start the next round!

Type: Arts and Crafts
Materials needed: a recipe and the items that the recipe calls for
Number of players: 2 or more

Ask a parent to help you with this one. Find a fun recipe, or use the one on page 54, "Make an Icy Treat!" Follow the recipe, noticing how important it is to do everything in the exact order in which the recipe tells you.

 *Study Right*

Show your kid how important it is to do things in the right order. If you have to run a bunch of errands, make a list. Put all the items in the order in which you plan to do them. Number them. Share this list with your kid and have a conversation about the order. You might say, "Why am I going to the grocery store last?" You might explain that you don't want the milk to go bad in the car, so you will get that last. This shows that sequence is something that you regularly think about, and they should too. The next time you go out, you might have your kid help you write your errand list.

Using Your Head

*Grab a **pencil**!*

Put yourself in Keisha's shoes!

Think of an object that you use every day. This might be a backpack you take to school every day or a pair of shoes you wear every day. Then, pretend that you don't know where it is. Retrace your steps, just as Keisha did.

List the last three times you saw this object. Make sure you put these in the correct order. Use the graphic organizer below to help you.

Missing Object	Last 3 Times I Saw It	Where the Object Is Now

Problem and Solution

In identifying a problem in a passage, kids this age sometimes pick things that they just don't like. Sometimes it's something that troubles them in their own lives. For example, when reading a passage in which a character wakes up on a Saturday morning to see rain, your kid might think rain is a problem (perhaps because your kid would want to play baseball and can't in the rain). But this isn't necessarily a problem in the passage. If the character in the passage works on a farm and the plants need rain, then the rain is definitely not a problem. Encourage your child to try to see things from the perspective of the character in the passage.

Kids this age are also focused on issues of fairness and insecurity. Pay close attention to what your child notices as a problem in a passage, and make sure that her choices reflect the details in the passage and not her internal logic.

First things first: Get a sense of what your kid already knows. Turn the page and tell your kid to Jump Right In!

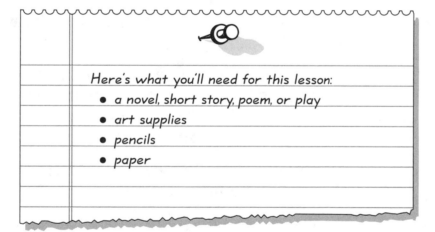

Here's what you'll need for this lesson:
- a novel, short story, poem, or play
- art supplies
- pencils
- paper

 **Jump Right In!**

Celeste the Figure Skater

My name is Celeste, and I have a lot of guts. At least that's what everyone tells me. I am a figure skater, and yesterday I competed at a big regional competition. Nothing went as planned. My morning practice was awful. I missed everything!

Afterwards, my coach, Mr. Allen, told me not to try the triple loop in the competition. "It's way too risky. Just do a double loop," he said.

"But I know I can land it, Mr. Allen," I pleaded, but he wouldn't budge.

"Maybe I'll just try it," I said to myself. "But what'll happen if I disobey Mr. Allen?" The rest of the day, all I could think about was the triple loop and Mr. Allen.

When I got to the rink that evening, more things went wrong. Taffy McQueen had claimed the entire locker room for herself. "I have all these brushes and dresses and dumbbells," she said. "You'll have to stretch by the candy machines."

As if that wasn't bad enough, right before I took the ice, I noticed that a button had fallen off my dress!

"Don't worry," Mr. Allen said, reaching in his coat pocket. "I've got glue. I can fix it." Mr. Allen was always ready for anything.

Once the button was back on, I skated to center ice and waited for my music to begin. The triple loop was the first jump I had planned. I skated in a big circle, getting myself ready for the jump. "I'm going to do it!" I thought to myself. "I'm going to prove to Mr. Allen that I can land this jump."

I had just the right amount of speed. I went up and—*bam!* I landed it! The crowd cheered, and a huge smile covered my face.

When I saw Mr. Allen afterward, I thought he was going to be mad, but he wasn't. "I knew you would land the jump," he said, "especially if I told you not to try it." He winked, and then added, "You've got guts, Celeste."

1. What problem arises between Celeste and Taffy McQueen?

   A. Taffy tells Celeste not to try the triple loop jump.

   B. Taffy does not want to share any of her brushes with Celeste.

   C. Taffy does not believe Celeste should be at the competition.

   D. Taffy does not want to share the locker room with Celeste.

2. When Celeste loses a button from her dress, how is this problem solved?

   A. Taffy offers one of her dresses.

   B. Mr. Allen glues the button back on.

   C. Celeste quickly changes her dress.

   D. Mr. Allen gives her extra time to fix the dress.

3. What problem arises between Celeste and Mr. Allen?

   _____

   _____

4. How does this problem get solved in the story?

   _____

   _____

Excellent Job!

 *Checking In*

Answers for page 105:

1. D

2. B

3. An A+ answer: "Mr. Allen tells Celeste not to try the triple loop jump in the competition. Celeste wants to try it anyway."

4. An A+ answer: "Celeste tries the jump in the competition. It turns out that Mr. Allen is not mad at her. He knew she would land it if he told her not to try it."

Did your child choose the correct answers? If so, ask your kid to underline the details that he used and have him explain all the problems in this passage.

Did your child get any answers wrong? If so, ask, "Why did you choose that answer?" Maybe your child followed her own thoughts and did not pay close enough attention to the information in the passage. For example, with question 2, your child might have thought that it would be nice if Taffy gave Celeste one of her brushes, so this answer could be appealing. But in the story this doesn't happen. You could say, "That's a good try, but did you use information from the passage to find your answer?" Go over the story with her and discuss together the conflicts that arise.

 *Watch Out!*

Sometimes your fourth grader follows his own likes and dislikes in answering these questions. For example, he might not like Celeste; perhaps he thinks Celeste is arrogant. Therefore, he might think that the conflict in question 3 arises from her arrogance—ignoring important details in the passage. You might say, "She might seem arrogant to you, but other kids might think she's confident." To help him identify the problem, say, "Try to word the problem as something that happens between Celeste and Mr. Allen. What does Celeste think or do, and what does Mr. Allen think or do that makes a problem?" By guiding him to name characters' thoughts or actions, you can help him stick to the details he is given in the passage.

What to Know...

Identifying the central problem in a story means identifying the most important problem the author created, not just the one most interesting to the reader. Make sure your kid can back up his or her answers with evidence from the passage.

Review these skills with your child this way:

- A **problem** in a passage may be between a character and another character, between a character and society, between a character and nature, or between a character and himself or herself. Sometimes there is a problem between opposing groups of characters.
- Sometimes a problem is called a **conflict.**

Your child might come across a paragraph like this in his or her reading:

Paul was mad at his brother Bruce. The two brothers shared a bike, but Bruce did not take good care of it. He rode it through mud and left it outside at night. He spilled ice cream on the seat and let the dog chew the tire. Paul didn't say anything because he was too nice. He knew that Bruce would get cranky and mad, and he didn't want to deal with that. So he just pretended everything was okay. The bike was a mess, though, and no one could ride it. So Paul eventually cleaned the ice cream off the seat so it wouldn't be sticky and changed the tire that the dog chewed. At least this way he could get some use out of the bike.

Ask your child to identify the biggest problem in the story. Then, ask him or her to identify some other problems in the story as well as any of Paul's solutions.

 *Checking In*

Kids should be able to identify the following problems in the story:

- The biggest problem is that Bruce doesn't take good care of their bike, and his brother Paul is mad about it.
- Another problem is that the bike is a mess, and no one could ride it.
- Another problem is that Paul won't say anything to Bruce.

Your kid should be able to identify the following solutions:

- Paul cleans the ice cream off the seat.
- Paul changes the busted tire so he can ride the bike.

Your kid might also be able to identify how these problems are set up:

- The first problem is between two characters, Paul and Bruce.
- The second problem is between a character and an object—in this case, the bike.
- The third problem is between a character and himself.

Fourth Graders Are...

Kids this age need breaks. A few minutes of exercise—jumping jacks, skipping rope, or playing games like tag or hide-and-seek—will work wonders. It will give them the energy to focus on their work. They will return to the activities with renewed energy and enthusiasm.

On Your Way to an "A" Activities

[45 minutes]

Type: Game/Competitive
Materials needed: paper and pencils
Number of players: 2 or more

Think of this activity as a friendly competition. Everyone should write a problem on a piece of paper. This should be one sentence, such as, "My science journal is missing" or "My homework blew away in the wind." Then, put all the papers in a pile. Each player should pick one. (If there are only two of you, simply trade papers.) Then, write a story that includes this problem. Be sure to include a solution too. Spend 30 minutes writing, and have fun with it. Then, read your stories out loud. Who did the best job including the problem in the story? Come up with a cool reward for that person.

[15 minutes]

Type: Arts and Crafts
Materials needed: art supplies and a novel, short story, poem, or play
Number of players: 2 or more

Read a fictional story in which a character has a problem. You might choose a novel, short story, poem, or even a play. Identify the biggest problem in the story. Then, draw a picture that shows the character facing this problem. Then, draw a picture that shows the character solving this problem. Hang your two pictures side by side on the wall.

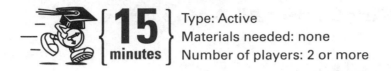

Type: Active
Materials needed: none
Number of players: 2 or more

Work with a partner on this one. Think of a problem, and then act out a scene in which you solve it. You might choose one of these problems: "My bike got a flat tire on the way to school" or "I lost my lunch money during recess." Start with the problem, and then solve it with your partner. Can you think of more than one way to solve each problem?

Type: Reading/Writing
Materials needed: pencils and paper
Number of players: 2 or more

Pretend that your morning is a story. Begin with the moment you woke up, and end with the moment you left your house. What problems did you face? Did you wake up late? Was there enough milk for your cereal? Could you find your shoes? Make a list. Leave a few blank lines between each problem. Which problem was the biggest? Circle that one. Now, think about the solutions. How did you solve each of these problems? Write the solutions under the problems.

 Study Right

Help your child identify problems and solutions. You might take a piece of paper and fold it vertically in half. This creates two columns. You can label one column "problems" and the other column "solutions." Write down some problems you face from day to day, and then write down the solutions. This will also help your kid distinguish between the two.

Using Your Head

*Grab some **paper** and a **pencil**!*

In "Celeste the Figure Skater," you learned about the problems that Celeste faced on the day of her competition. Celeste mentioned her problems with the triple loop jump, the locker room, and even her button. She also described the conflict she faced with her coach, Mr. Allen.

She didn't tell you that Taffy McQueen also faced a lot of problems. What problems do you think Taffy faced? Imagine some problems she might have had. Then, make a list of them.

You might write, "The lace on Taffy's skate broke while she was skating." Or, you might write, "Taffy worried that her program was boring."

In your list, include:

- one problem she has with Celeste
- one problem she has with the other skaters or coaches
- one problem she has with the rink or the ice on which she must skate
- one problem she has with herself
- at least one solution to any of these problems

After you have finished your list, pick the most interesting one. Write a few paragraphs in which you describe this problem as well as how Taffy solves it. For extra fun, pretend that you are Taffy when you describe the problem—and tell the story in her voice.

Comparing and Contrasting

Kids this age might feel overwhelmed by the sheer number of details that come at them in a passage. It can be a lot—especially if the author is describing two things side by side. It's challenging for kids to remember which details connect with what in a passage. Sometimes it's hard for us to do too, but you have to make sure your kid understands that he or she can always come back to the passage to double-check a detail. It's not going anywhere.

Returning to the passage is always a good idea. Sometimes, tiny differences in description can slide by on the first reading. One character might have long red hair, and another character might have short red hair. On a first reading, a kid might think, "They have the same hair." But if your kid returns to the passage, the similarities and differences become clear. Taking time to make sense of all the details can help to make the story easier to understand.

First things first: Get a sense of what your kid already knows. Turn the page and tell your kid to Jump Right In!

Here's what you'll need for this lesson:
- art supplies, such as crayons or markers
- paper

 **Jump Right In!**

Felix and Phillip

Last Saturday, I hung out with my two best friends, Felix and Phillip. They are so different. Felix is tall, runs faster than anyone I know, and can name all fifty states in fifty-eight seconds. Phillip is short, hates sports, and knows the name of every president but can't remember what state he lives in.

Last Saturday, we spent the entire morning in Felix's backyard. We played Frisbee, freeze tag, and badminton on the freshly mowed grass. Even Phillip seemed to have fun. "I don't mind these kinds of sports," he said, as we rested under a big apple tree. "I don't have to worry about dropping any ball or getting picked last."

We all laughed. Phillip is very easygoing and has a great sense of humor. He is always cracking jokes. Felix and I are more serious.

"You did great with the Frisbee," I said.

"Thanks, Tomo!" Phillip answered, smiling.

I think he thought I was just being nice, but he did really well. I dropped the Frisbee more than anyone else!

In the afternoon we went to Phillip's house. It started raining, so we stayed inside. His father brought us some snacks, and we played games in the family room. We played Go Fish over and over—and Felix seemed to win most of the time. "I get lucky a lot," Felix said, while sitting on the shaggy orange carpet. "If we played tomorrow, maybe I'd lose."

"Next Saturday, let's hang out at Tomo's house," Phillip said. "We can play Go Fish again."

"You're on!" I answered.

1. In what way are Felix and Phillip different?
   A. Phillip is tall, and Felix is short.
   B. Felix is tall, and Phillip is short.
   C. Phillip likes sports, and Felix does not.
   D. Felix always makes jokes, and Phillip is more serious.

2. When the three boys play Go Fish, they are
   A. in Felix's backyard
   B. outside Phillip's house
   C. under an apple tree
   D. in Phillip's family room

3. In what way are Felix and Tomo different from Phillip?

   _____

   _____

   _____

4. When the three boys get together next Saturday, what will be different? What will be the same?

   _____

   _____

   _____

   _____

Excellent Job!

 **Checking In**

Ⓐ Answers for page 115:

1. B

2. D

3. An A+ answer: "Felix and Tomo are more serious than Phillip. Phillip is always cracking jokes."

4. An A+ answer: "When the three boys get together next Saturday, they will be at Tomo's house. This means that the place will be different. They will play Go Fish again. This is something that will remain the same."

Did your child choose the correct answers? If so, tell your child to underline the details that she used. Have her explain how these details show similarities and differences.

Did your child get any of the answers wrong? Maybe he mixed up some of the details from the passage. For example, if your child wrote that Felix and Tomo are goofy and always cracking jokes as an answer for question 3, this shows that he mixed up the description of Phillip with the other boys. You could say, "That's a good try, but did you check your answers against the information in the passage?" Go over the passage and have him underline details and connect each detail to the person or event it describes.

 **Watch Out!**

Sometimes fourth graders have trouble keeping details straight. This is understandable, especially if a passage is full of details. In the first paragraph of this passage, your kid learns a lot about Felix and Phillip. She shouldn't try to memorize these details. This would take too long, and it's unnecessary. Instead, encourage her to have a general understanding of what the details convey—in this case, that Felix and Phillip are very different. Then, remind her that she can always return to the passage to answer a specific question. So, to answer question 1, your kid would want to reread the first paragraph. Which character is tall? Which is short? The passage spells it out.

What to Know...

Your kid might be confused by the words *comparing* and *contrasting*. He or she can also understand these skills in terms of what is similar and what is different.

Review these skills with your child this way:

- **Comparing** is noting what is similar between two or more ideas, characters, details, or events in a passage.
- **Contrasting** is noting what is different between two or more ideas, characters, details, or events in a passage.
- Children can use the words *similar* and *different*.

Your child comes across things that are the same and things that are different every day. Your child might see the following on a menu:

Ask your child to identify some ways in which the three lunches are similar. Then, ask for differences. You might be specific and ask, "How is Lunch 2 different from Lunch 1?"

Kids should be able to identify the similarities among the lunches:

- All three lunches include water.
- All three lunches include a salad.
- Lunch 2 and Lunch 3 both include garlic bread.
- Lunch 1 and Lunch 2 both include soda.

There are many differences, and kids should be able to identify some of these too:

- Lunch 1 includes a hamburger, but the other two lunches do not.
- Lunch 2 includes pizza, but the other two lunches do not.
- Lunch 3 includes vegetable soup, but the other two lunches do not.

 **Study Right**

Comparing and contrasting two things can help your kid develop strong reading comprehension. When you are at the store trying to decide between two items, ask your kid to list the ways that they are similar and different. You might choose two different cereals and include any differences in the prices, the nutritional value, or the number of servings. Which item did you choose? Talk about your decision with your kid. Show him or her how the list helped you.

Fourth Graders Are...

Kids this age often enjoy being in clubs and doing activities and sports. If your kid is working with friends on these activities, you might encourage them to come up with a name for themselves. Being part of a club—especially one with a cool name—can make these activities even more fun.

On Your Way to an "A" Activities

30 { minutes }

Type: Arts and Crafts
Materials needed: art supplies and paper
Number of players: 2 or more

Draw two pictures of the same thing. You might draw a picture of a house with the family and pets standing out front, or you might draw a picture of some kids having a picnic in the park. When you draw the second picture, make sure that some details are slightly different. For example, the house might not have a chimney in the second picture. Or maybe the cat is all black instead of orange. Be sure to keep some details the same. Share your pictures with others. Can they spot the similarities and the differences?

30 { minutes }

Type: Game/Competitive
Materials needed: none
Number of players: 2

Choose a room in the house. You and a partner should walk around this room and notice as many details as you can. Then, one of you should leave the room, and the other should stay. The player who stays should make small changes all over the room. This player might move an alarm clock to another table, switch the pillows on the bed, or place a stuffed animal on a different shelf. Then, the other player should return to the room. How many differences can this player detect in one minute? Switch roles, and try this again.

Using Your Head

{ 30 minutes }

*Grab a **pencil!***

The next week, the three boys got together again and Felix described their day. Read what he wrote. Then, answer the questions.

Phillip, Tomo, and I usually hang out together on Saturdays. I've known Phillip since I was five, but I met Tomo last year. Tomo does really well in school, but he and Phillip both can't remember the names of the states. Tomo has trouble remembering Arizona and Arkansas. He runs really fast! He's like the wind. This really surprised me because he's not very tall.

This past week, we hung out at Tomo's house. We played Go Fish in his family's kitchen, and his mother made us some chocolate chip cookies. The sun was shining through the window, making the room seem really bright. I'm really lucky to have such great friends like Phillip and Tomo.

1. The three boys play Go Fish in both passages. What things are different during each of the games?

   _____

   _____

2. In what ways are Felix and Tomo similar? In what ways are they different?

   _____

   _____

Cause and Effect

Kids this age have a habit of racing through passages. They might jump to a conclusion about a cause-and-effect relationship without using evidence from the passage. They might answer with the first thing that comes to mind, or they might base their answer on something that is happening in their own lives. They shouldn't think of reading as a race. If your kid reads carefully, he or she will make fewer mistakes.

First things first: Get a sense of what your kid already knows. Turn the page and tell your kid to Jump Right In!

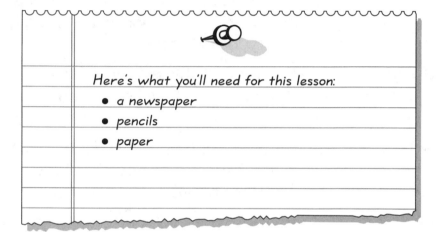

Here's what you'll need for this lesson:
- a newspaper
- pencils
- paper

 **Jump Right In!**

The Mystery at Crooked Steps Inn

Marnie was determined to solve the mystery at Crooked Steps Inn. The inn belonged to her Aunt Ivy, and her parents had always told her that "funny things" happened there. One time, a guest's locket disappeared in the middle of the night. Another time, the candles in the hallway suddenly blew out—and nobody was near them. Another time, the big French doors in the living room slammed shut, startling everyone in the room.

Marnie had always heard stories like this and wanted to investigate. She loved reading Nancy Drew books, and she wanted to be a sleuth too.

Marnie's father was planning to visit his sister Ivy for her birthday, so this was Marnie's chance. "Take me with you, Dad!" she pleaded. "I want to be like Nancy Drew!"

"All right, Marnie," he answered. "But don't pester Aunt Ivy about these mysteries."

When Marnie and her father arrived at the inn, Marnie immediately noticed the crooked steps leading up to the front porch. "Those steps look creepy," Marnie whispered.

Her father laughed. "While the builders were laying the bricks, a huge lightning storm started," he explained. "They all ran inside—and then went home for the day. When they returned, the cement had dried, and the bricks were all crooked."

Marnie's father rang the doorbell. Aunt Ivy opened the door and greeted them with open arms. Her long black dress touched the floor and hid her feet.

"Marnie," Aunt Ivy said, once they were in the living room. "You should know that this house is full of secret staircases. If you slide that bookcase over there to the left, a narrow set of stairs appears. Those lead to my bedroom."

"Wow," said Marnie, glancing at her father.

"You've got your work cut out for you, Nancy!" he said with a smile. "Oops, I mean Marnie."

1. Why do Marnie and her father visit Aunt Ivy?

    A. Marnie's father wants Aunt Ivy to sell the old inn.

    B. Aunt Ivy wants to solve the mystery of her inn.

    C. Marnie's father promised to take Marnie to the inn.

    D. It is Aunt Ivy's birthday.

2. What happens if someone slides the bookcase in the inn's living room to the left?

    A. The candles in the hallway blow out.

    B. The French doors in the living room slam shut.

    C. A staircase to Aunt Ivy's bedroom appears.

    D. A secret passage to the kitchen is blocked.

3. Why are the steps leading up to Aunt Ivy's inn crooked?

    _____

    _____

    _____

Excellent Job!

 **Checking In**

Ⓐ Answers for page 123:

1. D

2. C

3. An A+ answer: "The steps leading up to the inn are crooked because the builders had to stop working when a lightning storm began. When they returned to work, the cement had dried and the steps were crooked."

Did your child choose the correct answers? If so, you could play a game with your kid where you name a cause and your kid identifies the effect.

Did your child get any of the answers wrong? If so, ask, "Did you rush through the story?" Maybe your kid didn't use information from the story. If so, you could go back over the story together and have him or her underline each cause and what effects came from these events.

 **Watch Out!**

Sometimes fourth graders don't return to the passage to determine the correct answer. They blaze through their work, and this causes them to make mistakes. Encourage your kid to return to the passage if he or she does not know the answer right off the bat. The story isn't going anywhere, and the details he or she needs to identify the correct answers are all in the passage.

What to Know...

Some kids have trouble distinguishing between cause and effect. Or they have trouble identifying the specific details that lead to one or the other.

Review these skills with your child this way:

- The **cause** is the reason an event happens.
- The **effect** is the result of an event, feeling, or idea.

Your child might have to follow rules such as these in his or her classroom.

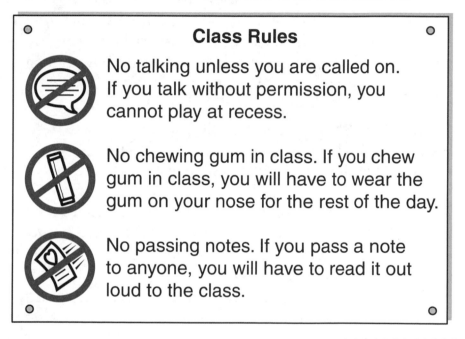

Class Rules

No talking unless you are called on. If you talk without permission, you cannot play at recess.

No chewing gum in class. If you chew gum in class, you will have to wear the gum on your nose for the rest of the day.

No passing notes. If you pass a note to anyone, you will have to read it out loud to the class.

Ask your child to identify the causes and effects in these rules. You might give him an effect and ask him to identify the cause.

 *Checking In*

Your kid should be able to determine different cause-and-effect relationships in these rules:

- Cause: Talking in class. Effect: You will not be able to play at recess.
- Cause: Chewing gum in class. Effect: You will have to wear the gum on your nose for the rest of the day.
- Cause: Passing a note in class. Effect: You will have to read your note out loud.

On Your Way to an "A" Activities

30 minutes

Type: Speaking/Listening
Materials needed: a newspaper
Number of players: 2 or more

Choose an interesting article in the newspaper. Read the article, paying close attention to cause-and-effect relationships. Then, one player should offer a statement that is a cause or an effect from the article. If it is a cause, then the others should identify the effect. If it is an effect, then the others should come up with the cause. See how many you can come up with for one article. Then, try another article.

15 minutes

Type: Reading/Writing
Materials needed: pencils and paper
Number of players: 2 or more

Tell the other player(s) things about yourself using a series of cause-and-effect statements. You can use the word *because* to connect the effect with the cause. For example, you might write, "I am a very good speller because I like to read a lot" or "I don't like cats because I always sneeze when I'm around them." Come up with at least 10 cause-and-effect statements. Read them aloud.

Fourth Graders Are...

Cause-and-effect statements create order in the world. They spell out the reasons that something happens—or they pinpoint the effects of something. This might appeal to your kid. Help your kid think of determining cause and effect in a passage as a fun game.

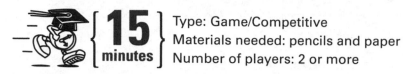

Type: Game/Competitive
Materials needed: pencils and paper
Number of players: 2 or more

Everyone should have a piece of paper. Fold the paper in half down the center. Then, write the word *because* at the top. On the left, write a *cause*. On the right, write the *effect* that goes with it. For example, you might write, "I get home from school at three because school gets out at two-thirty." Or, you might write, "My dad takes the bus to work because we only have one car." How many statements can each person come up with in five minutes?

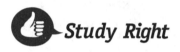 **Study Right**

The word *because* can be very useful in helping your kid understand a cause-and-effect relationship. *Because* reveals the cause of an effect. For example, "I am out of breath because I ran all the way home." Encourage your kid to use the word *because* to separate and understand cause-and-effect relationships.

Has your child breezed through the activities? If so, he or she can work on this Using Your Head activity independently.

Using Your Head

Grab a **pencil**!

Back at the Crooked Steps Inn, it was bedtime. Marnie wanted an extra blanket, so she looked in the closet, where she discovered something strange. There was a painting propped against the wall, and when she looked behind it she found a dusty hardcover book. Marnie opened it up and began to read.

"The Winchester Mystery House is a strange mansion in northern California. Its owner ordered carpenters to work on the mansion around the clock. It is a huge house with staircases that lead to the ceiling and doors that open to nothing! Outside, it has beautiful gardens. The house still stands today. It is so big that painters must always paint it. As soon as the last parts are painted, it is time to start painting again."

1. What happens to Marnie because she enters the closet??

_____

_____

2. Why are painters always painting the mansion?

_____

_____

Answers: 1. Marnie discovers a book about the Winchester Mystery House. 2. Painters must always paint the mansion because it is so big. As soon as they are done, it is time to start again!

Fact and Opinion

Kids this age are pretty familiar with the terms *fact* and *opinion,* but sometimes they have a hard time recognizing facts. They think of facts as things they *know*—even if the statements are opinions. So, they might think that "Grandma is nice" is a fact because they *know* it to be true. While most people probably do think that Grandma is nice, it's possible that there are people out there who don't feel this way. Or kids might think that "Math is hard" is a fact, when there definitely are people who don't think math is hard. Make sure your kid understands that both of those statements are opinions, and that facts are things that can be proven to be true by everyone.

First things first: Get a sense of what your kid already knows. Turn the page and tell your kid to Jump Right In!

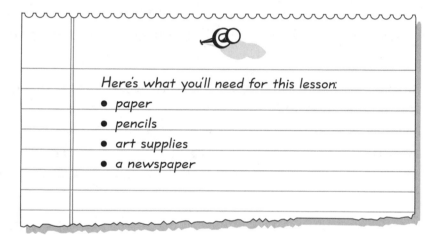

Here's what you'll need for this lesson:
- *paper*
- *pencils*
- *art supplies*
- *a newspaper*

Jump Right In!

Ari's Secret

Ari had a secret life. Everyone at school knew he loved soccer and pizza. They knew he earned a certificate for perfect attendance last year and that his sister Rachel was in the eighth grade. They knew he liked English and could do more chin-ups than anyone else during recess. They knew he was kind.

They didn't know what he did after school every Monday and Wednesday. They didn't know that he volunteered two hours of his time twice a week. They didn't know that he helped someone who really needed his help.

On those two days, he went to Ms. Song's house down the street. She was 93 and had trouble seeing. She couldn't stand up for more than a few minutes without her cane, but she was fun to be around. She was funny and thoughtful. She had a sweet voice and wore a flower in her hair every day. She always asked interesting questions.

Ari read her mail and parts of the newspaper to her. Sometimes he made some phone calls for her. One time, he canceled a magazine subscription for her. Another time, he confirmed a doctor's appointment for her. He even fixed the clock on her stove after the electricity went out. Ari helped Ms. Song with very interesting things.

Most importantly, Ari gave her some company. He asked her how she was, and he told her what was going on at his school. She loved hearing what Mr. Kulik, his teacher, had said. They talked about television shows. They both watched *American Idol* and rooted for the same contestants. They had a good time together.

Ari never told anyone at school about Ms. Song because he liked having a secret. He knew that his teacher would make a big deal about it and tell everyone that he was doing a very good deed. Ari didn't care about that. He wanted to do this because he wanted to help Ms. Song. He knew that she appreciated him, and that was enough.

1. Which of these statements is a *fact*?

   A. Ms. Song asked interesting questions.

   B. Ms. Song had a sweet voice.

   C. Ms. Song was 93.

   D. Ms. Song was funny.

2. Which of these statements is an *opinion*?

   A. Ari confirmed a doctor's appointment for Ms. Song.

   B. Ari helped Ms. Song with very interesting things.

   C. Ari read Ms. Song's mail to her.

   D. Ari canceled a magazine subscription for Ms. Song.

3. In the first paragraph, the passage states that Ari was kind. Is this a fact or an opinion? Explain your answer.

   _____

   _____

4. In the last paragraph, the passage states that Ari never told anyone at school about Ms. Song. Is this a fact or an opinion? Explain your answer.

   _____

   _____

Excellent Job!

 *Checking In*

Answers for page 131:

1. C

2. B

3. An A+ answer: "This is an opinion. It is the belief of the author of this passage. Someone else might disagree with this statement. No one can prove this statement to be true."

4. An A+ answer: "This is a fact. It can be proven to be true. Someone can confirm that Ari never told anyone at school about Ms. Song."

Did your child pick the correct answers? If so, ask your child to explain his or her choices. Ask, "Why is that a fact?" or "Why is that an opinion?"

Did your child get any of the answers wrong? If so, ask, "Could someone disagree with that?" Maybe your child is not clear on what a fact or an opinion is. You might want to go over all of the facts and opinions in the story with him and have him explain his understanding of what makes a fact a fact. Sometimes, things that sound like facts are well-disguised opinions. For example, things like personality traits, such as Ari's kindness in question 3, are hard to prove true all of the time.

 *Watch Out!*

Sometimes fourth graders think that a fact is something that they believe to be true. The statement "Ari is kind" might seem like a fact because all of the information in the passage supports it, but it is still an opinion. If one person can disagree with the statement, then it is an opinion.

What to Know...

Kids can have trouble distinguishing facts from opinions. The most important thing is that they understand that a fact is something that is always true, while an opinion cannot be proven true in all cases.

Review these skills with your child this way:

- **Facts** are statements that are true. Facts can be about people, places, numbers, and many other things. Facts can be proven to be true.

- **Opinions** are beliefs or judgments held by a person or a group. Opinions may be supported by information, but they cannot be proven to be true.

Your child may read a movie review on the Internet such as this.

http://www.zoinks.com

The movie *Zoinks!* is fantastic! It follows the adventures of a dog named Zoinks. This dog is special. He lives with the Adams family and helps them when they face problems. He saves their cat from another dog. He protects the kids at the park. He even fetches the newspaper in the morning. Zoinks is incredible. You'll love him!

Ask your child to identify some facts and opinions in the movie review. Make sure your child can tell you why each statement is a fact or an opinion.

 *Checking In*

Kids should be able to identify the following facts:

- The film follows the adventures of a dog named Zoinks.
- Zoinks lives with the Adams family.
- Zoinks saves the family's cat from another dog.
- Zoinks protects the kids at the park.
- Zoinks fetches the newspaper in the morning.

They should also be able to identify the following opinions:

- The movie *Zoinks!* is fantastic.
- Zoinks is special.
- Zoinks is incredible.
- You'll love Zoinks.

 *Study Right*

Kids this age are often very talkative. They like to explain things. If this is true for your kid, then encourage it as a way to help her learn new skills. Movie reviews and book reviews are a good mix of facts and opinions. Next time you read one with your kid, talk about the facts and the opinions. You might ask your kid to explain why a statement is a fact or an opinion. This will help her grasp these terms, while satisfying her desire to be expressive. You should point out that opinions are often supported by facts.

On Your Way to an "A" Activities

Type: Speaking/Listening
Materials needed: none
Number of players: 2 or more

Think of someone all the players know. This might be someone famous or someone in your class at school. Describe this person using five statements that are facts. For example, imagine you chose figure skater Michelle Kwan. You might say, "Michelle Kwan went to the Olympics" or "She is from California." Then, describe this person using five opinions. For Michelle Kwan, you might say, "She is a beautiful skater."

Type: Arts and Crafts
Materials needed: paper and art supplies, such as crayons, markers, glitter, felt
Number of players: 2 or more

This activity builds on the one above. Go back to the person you described. Think of the five facts and five opinions you came up with. Now, create two pictures of this person. The first picture should reflect all five of the *facts*. The second picture should reflect all five of the *opinions*. How are the two pictures different?

Using Your Head

{15 minutes}

*Grab a **pencil**!*

One of the letters that Ari read to Ms. Song was from her daughter Kyun. Read Kyun's letter. Then, answer the questions that follow.

Dear Mom,

You are so thoughtful. I am happy to have your recipe for tomato soup. I will make it for the kids this week. I know they will love it, and I will tell them that it was your recipe. My garden is growing fast and takes up the entire area next to the garage. The tomatoes will be ready soon. I will send you pictures!

Love,

Kyun

1. Identify a fact in the letter. What makes this a fact?

_____

_____

2. Identify an opinion in the letter. What makes this an opinion?

_____

_____

Answers: 1. A fact is that the garden takes up the entire area next to the garage. This can be proven to be true. No one can disagree. 2. An opinion is that Ms. Song is thoughtful and kind. Someone might disagree with this. It cannot be proven to be true.

Theme

The term *theme* might be new to most kids. They might confuse the concept with the main idea or the summary of a passage. But theme is different. Theme is the big idea expressed by a story. It might not be stated within the story, which can make it harder to pin down. However, when kids step back from a text and say what they learned from it in their own words, this is usually pretty close to the theme.

In the classroom, your kid will be asked to identify themes in stories and poems, so it's good to give him or her practice with this concept.

First things first: Get a sense of what your kid already knows. Turn the page and tell your kid to Jump Right In!

Here's what you'll need for this lesson:
- art supplies
- old magazines
- a book of poems
- paper
- pencils

Jump Right In!

Maria and the Math Test

Maria settled into her seat. "This is hard!" she thought to herself. She had missed two weeks of school when she had the chicken pox, and now she had to take a math test after school. Her teacher, Mr. Casteel, was correcting her classmates' tests at his desk. She could see that he was marking a lot of answers wrong with his red pen.

"Maria," Mr. Casteel said. "I have to step out to speak with the principal. I'll be back in ten minutes."

"Okay, Mr. Casteel," Maria answered, looking up from her test.

When Mr. Casteel left, Maria realized that the answer key to the test was on his desk. It would have been so easy to look at the answers. Maria thought about it for a brief moment, but then she continued working on her test.

"I may not do very well on this test," she said to herself, "but at least I'll know I was honest."

1. What is the theme of this story?

_____

_____

2. Which of these titles best reflects the theme of the story?

A. Trust Your Parents

B. Stay in School

C. Honesty Is Best

D. Math Is Hard

Will's Love

When Will walked up the walkway
To his house
His head whirled
With worries.

His teacher yelled at him.
His friends were mad.
Even his dog growled at him.
He wanted a hug.

But when he opened the door
And saw his little sister's face—
So sad as she sat on the sofa,
He knew he could forget all that.

She needed that hug
And he would be the one to give it.
He would be the big brother
Because he had a big heart.

3. What is the theme of this poem?

_____

_____

4. Which of these titles best reflects the theme of the poem?

A. Will Comes Home

B. Being a Big Brother

C. Turn the Other Cheek

D. The Sun Will Shine Again

Excellent Job!

 *Checking In*

Ⓐ Answers for pages 138 and 139:

1. An A+ answer: "A girl realizes that it's important to be honest."

2. C

3. An A+ answer: "Having a big heart means caring for other people, even when you want to be cared for yourself."

4. B

Did your child choose the correct answers? If so, ask your child to explain how he came to figure out the themes and how the other possible titles don't quite capture what each passage is dealing with.

Did your child get any of the questions wrong? If so, ask, "Why did you pick that answer?" Maybe your child picked the title that seemed most interesting. For example, with question 4, the third answer shows something that someone with a big heart would probably do, but it doesn't fit with the events in the story. Ask your kid how she would describe the story (or poem) to someone else. Can your kid go from talking about the content to identifying the broader theme?

 *Watch Out!*

Sometimes fourth graders confuse *theme* with *main idea* and *summary*. If your kid is not clear on the differences, you might want to revisit the material on *summary* from pages 45 to 52 and the material on *main idea* from pages 71 to 78. To clear up some of the confusion, you could say, "A summary briefly retells the most important information in a passage. It might be a few sentences or even a paragraph in length. A main idea is usually one sentence and states what a passage is mostly about. These are both different from the theme. The theme is the big idea expressed by a story. Theme is often what you learned from a story." The theme isn't always right in front of your kid, so he may have to take some time to try and figure it out. For example in "The Three Little Pigs," the theme is that you should always build your house with solid building materials so that it will stand strong. But this is never outwardly stated. You might use other stories or poems your kid is familiar with and have him try to express what the author is trying to say throughout the story or poem.

What to Know...

Theme can seem like a fuzzy concept for kids this age. It's kind of abstract, and it may be hard for them to pin down. The most important thing is that your kid is clear on what the term means. If your child gets confused, he or she can always fall back on this definition.

Review this skill with your child this way:

- A **theme** is a big idea expressed by a story or poem.

Your child might encounter a poem such as this in his or her reading.

What Tim Learned

When I got to school
    with water dripping down
    my face
    with my new pants soaked
    and muddy
    and with my shirt sticking to
    my skin

I thought about what my mom had said:
    Bring your umbrella!

· · · · · · · · · · · · · ·

Ask your child to determine the theme of the poem. Have your child explain his or her answer. You could ask, "What do you think the author is really trying to say here?"

 *Checking In*

Kids should be able to identify the theme:

- It is a good idea to listen to your parents because they often know what's best.

Some kids might get confused and summarize the poem. If you find that your child says something like, "Tim got soaked going to school and thought about what his mom told him," wait for him or her to finish and then say, "That's a good summary, but now what do you think the *theme* is?"

On Your Way to an "A" Activities

30 minutes — Type: Arts and Crafts
Materials needed: paper, art supplies, old magazines
Number of players: 2 or more

Think of a story that you read and enjoyed, or read a new short story or poem. Then, ask yourself, "What is the theme expressed by this story or poem?" After you have identified the theme, create a collage that represents the theme. (Remember, a collage is a picture made with photographs, cloth, paper, and other objects.)

45 minutes — Type: Speaking/Listening
Materials needed: a book of poems
Number of players: 2 or more

Have some snacks with friends and then notice a couple of things that you learn from having snacks (like sharing food or saying thanks). Write a shared poem or a story where each player writes a line or a sentence about having snacks that slowly builds up to show a theme about sharing.

Type: Active
Materials needed: none
Number of players: 2 or more

Put on a play! Think about the theme from "Maria and the Math Test": Even though it's tempting to cheat, you'll feel better about yourself if you're honest. Or think about the theme from "Will's Love": Being a big-hearted person means caring for other people, even when you want to be cared for yourself. Now, put on a play that tells one of these themes to your audience. You can act out these stories, or you can come up with whatever story you'd like. If you want to use a theme from something else that you've read, that's okay too.

Type: Reading/Writing
Materials needed: paper and pencils
Number of players: 2 or more

Throughout this book, you have learned about main idea, summary, and theme. Choose a book, short story, or poem that you really like. Then, write down its main idea, its summary, and its theme. After you are done, look closely at what you wrote. How are they different?

 Study Right

Understanding the theme of a text is important to appreciating it. When your kid mentions that he or she enjoyed reading something, ask, "What did you learn from it?" From there, you can guide your kid to identify the theme. A story's lesson and its theme are often closely related.

Has your child breezed through the activities? If so, he or she can work on this Using Your Head activity independently.

Using Your Head

{ 45 }
minutes

*Grab a **pencil** and a **notebook**!*

Think of something you believe to be true. You might come up with something like, "It is important to recycle" or "We should all try to help people who are older." Write this statement down on a piece of paper. Call it your theme.

Now, write a short story or poem that uses this theme. You might write a story such as "Maria and the Math Test" or a poem such as "Will's Love." Make sure that what you write follows your theme, but remember, you don't have to come out and say it. Often, themes are not stated but are shown by what happens in the story or the poem.

Share what you wrote with others. Can they determine your theme without you telling them what it is?

Addition and Subtraction

Your kid uses addition and subtraction almost every day, whether he thinks about it or not. By fourth grade, your child has used addition to count his change and figure out how much money he has. Or he's used subtraction to figure out how many days of school are left before the next holiday.

Now, your child is facing higher-level problems in mathematics and needs to be able to apply these skills to succeed. But without addition and subtraction skills, your kid will have a hard time grasping concepts such as multiplication and division, not to mention more advanced mathematics.

You need to provide your kid with practice in adding and subtracting large, multi-digit numbers. This is what your kid will be working on in the classroom, so giving her adding and subtracting practice with large numbers at home will show her how she can use these skills in her life. It doesn't hurt for your kid to see how math class matters in the real world. Giving your kid manipulatives, games, and helpful tips can take the sting out of learning and help her master these skills.

First things first: Get a sense of what your kid already knows. Turn the page and tell your kid to Jump Right In!

Here's what you'll need for this lesson:
- *paper*
- *pencil*
- *dimes and pennies*
- *place markers*
- *2 index cards*

Although you may be more familiar with the terms *carrying* and *borrowing*, we will be using the term *regrouping* throughout the rest of the book. So, when you see the term *regroup*, you can think *carry* when adding and *borrow* when subtracting.

Jump Right In!

1. While playing a video game, you scored 3,574 points. Then, you saved the game to play later. The next time you played, you scored 422 more points. How many points did you score in all?

   A. 3,152   **C.** 3,998

   B. 3,996   **D.** 4,996

2. Of the 3,574 points you scored before you saved the game, 423 were bonus points. How many points did you get without the bonus points?

   A. 151   **C.** 3,151

   B. 3,141   **D.** 3,997

3. While playing your video game, you get points for finding swords and lightning bolts.

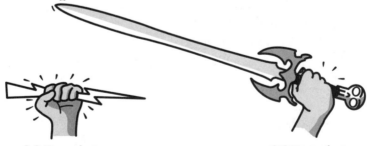

335 points   225 points

How many points would you get altogether for finding 2 swords and 1 lightning bolt?

_____

4. A town fair made $943 in ticket sales before noon on Saturday. After noon, the fair made an additional $6,674 in ticket sales. How much did the fair make in ticket sales that Saturday?

    A. $6,517

    B. $6,617

    C. $7,617

    D. $615,117

5. At the ringtoss booth at the fair, 1,206 people played. Of these, 127 won. How many people did <u>not</u> win?

    A. 1,029

    B. 1,079

    C. 1,121

    D. 1,189

For questions 6 and 7, write your answers as a sentence.

6. A library has 1,309 videos in the children's section and 790 movies in the teen section. How many videos are there in all?

_____

7. Of the 1,309 videos in the children's section, 846 are cartoons. How many videos are <u>not</u> cartoons?

_____

_____

Excellent Job!

 **Checking In**

Ⓐ Answers for pages 148 and 149:

1. B

2. C

3. An A+ answer. "I got 785 points altogether."

4. C

5. B

6. An A+ answer: "There are 2,099 videos altogether."

7. An A+ answer: "There are 463 videos that are not cartoons."

If your child answered correctly, ask her to show how she added (or subtracted) the numbers. Make sure that your kid picked the correct answer because she knew how to do the problem and wasn't guessing.

If your child answered incorrectly, review each question. Ask, "In question 4, the digits in the tens place are 4 and 7. What happened when you added 4 tens and 7 tens?" Explain that if he was counting on his fingers to add, he would run out of fingers. That means he needs to regroup. Encourage him to "count on." For example, to add 4 and 7, he starts at 7, and then "counts on": 8, 9, 10, 11. Here he has 11 tens that regroup to 1 hundred and 1 ten. Your kid should write a 1 above the hundreds place and a 1 in the tens place of the answer. Then, have your kid continue adding.

 **Watch Out!**

Your kid can practice regrouping by using coins. Line 3 dimes and 5 pennies above 2 dimes and 7 pennies. Write $0.35 + $0.27 on a piece of paper (vertically). Now, ask your kid to put all the pennies in a pile and add them. When she adds 5 pennies and 7 pennies, tell her that she can have only one digit in the "pennies" column of the answer—so she must regroup. Have her regroup 12 pennies for 1 dime and 2 pennies (she should give you 10 pennies in exchange for 1 dime and put this in the pile of dimes). Then, she can add all the dimes. Do the same for subtraction and have her regroup when she doesn't have enough pennies to subtract. Tell her to use **BBB** to know when to regroup when subtracting—**B**igger on **B**ottom then **B**orrow.

What to Know...

Your child can use addition and subtraction while at a store, while playing games, or even while on a trip. Your child learned these concepts early in school and will continue to build on these skills.

Review these skills with your child this way:

- **Addition** is an operation that combines numbers.
- The **sum** is a number that results from adding numbers.
- **Subtraction** is an operation on two numbers that tells the difference between the numbers.
- The **difference** is a number that results from subtracting a number from another number.

You and your child might map out a vacation route and add to find the total distance you'll travel.

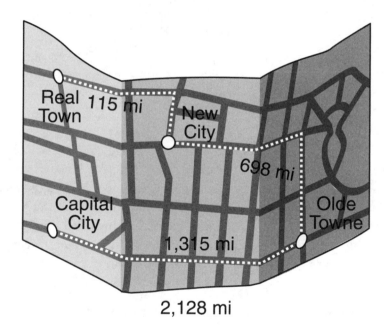

2,128 mi

Encourage your child to add the distances to check the total distance. As your child adds the distances, have him explain how he is regrouping aloud.

Your kid can also learn about how addition and subtraction are necessary when balancing a checkbook.

ABC Bank Statement

Original Balance $5,000

New Balance $3,200

Artie Jones
20 Washington Drive
Anywhere, USA 11002

Date: 6/10/06

Date: 6/10/06

To: Save the Foxes Foundation

$1,275

Amount: Five hundred Twenty,five & $\frac{00}{100}$ $525

Account Number: 188-500-329   Artie Jones

Total $1,800 . . . .

Ask your kid to add the two checks together to find the sum. Then, subtract to make sure the new balance is correct.

 ## Checking In

If your kid doesn't remember to regroup, ask, "What do you do if you have a larger number to subtract from a smaller number?" When subtracting $1,800 from $5,000, your child subtracts the ones (0 ones – 0 ones = 0 ones) and subtracts the tens (0 tens – 0 tens = 0 tens). Then, your child must regroup to subtract the hundreds. He can regroup 5 thousands into 4 thousands and 10 hundreds and then subtract the hundreds (10 hundreds – 8 hundreds = 2 hundreds). Finally, he can subtract the thousands (4 thousands – 1 thousand = 3 thousands) to get the answer $3,200.

 ## Study Right

Throughout these activities, make sure your kid is lining the digits up correctly. When students regroup while adding, make sure they write the *regrouped* digit in the correct column. When students regroup while subtracting, make sure they cross out the digit they are regrouping from and write the correct digit that remains so they can keep track.

On Your Way to an "A" Activities

{ 20 minutes }

Type: Game/Competitive
Materials needed: dice, index card, pencil
Number of players: 2 or more

Play a game of "Rolling Addition." The first person rolls a die (often called a number cube in school) six times and uses the numbers rolled to make two 3-digit numbers (the first number on the first roll will be the first digit in one number, and so on). Then, this player adds the two numbers. The second person rolls the number cube to make two 3-digit numbers in the same way, and adds the numbers. The person with the greatest sum gets a point. The first person to score 5 points wins the game.

{ 30 minutes }

Type: Game/Competitive
Materials needed: 2 index cards, place markers, paper, pencils
Number of players: 2 or more

Play a game of "Addition/Subtraction Baseball." Each person makes his or her playing field on an index card (consisting of 4 bases). One player pitches by writing an addition or subtraction problem. The other player bats by finding the sum or difference. If the answer is incorrect, that player gets one strike. If the answer is correct, the batter goes to first base. The game is continued in this way until the player gets 3 strikes and makes an out (then it's the other player's turn). Or the player keeps answering correct questions to advance around the bases. When a player gets to home base, the other player automatically gets a turn to bat. The first player to score 10 runs wins the game.

Has your child breezed through the activities? If so, he or she can work on this Using Your Head activity independently.

Using Your Head

{ **20** minutes }

*Grab some **paper**, a **pencil**, and a **die** (a number cube)!*

Roll the die four times. The numbers you rolled will determine how much money is in your bank account. Make the biggest number you can!

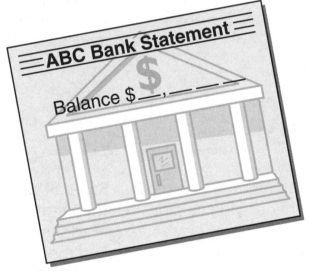

You want to give away some of your money to charity. Which charities will you donate to?

How much money will you send to each charity?

How much will you have left in your bank account?

Multiplication and Division

Fourth graders use multiplication and division all the time. They multiply when they count groups of the same kinds of coins and skip-count. They divide when they share a pizza or split up into groups to play games. Multiplication and division (along with addition and subtraction) are the skills that kids will continue to use all their lives and the skills they will use most in math.

Although many fourth graders generally know how to multiply and divide, many have a hard time with multiplication and division facts. Teachers expect students to memorize them, yet most kids find it difficult to remember what seem to be oh-so-many facts. Another difficulty with multiplication and division is the size of the numbers that the kids are expected to work with in school. Kids don't usually use large numbers in their everyday lives. They need lots of practice so that when they come across big numbers in the classroom, they won't get stumped.

To help your kid master multiplication and division skills, give him tricks that he can use to remember multiplication facts and a way out if he should get stuck working with large numbers.

First things first: Get a sense of what your kid already knows. Turn the page and tell your kid to Jump Right In!

Here's what you'll need for this lesson:
- *paper*
- *pencil*
- *marker*
- *index cards*

Jump Right In!

1. You're having a pizza party with your friends. You get 6 large pizzas for the party. Each pizza has 8 slices. How many slices of pizza are there in total?

   A. 14

   B. 36

   C. 40

   D. 48

2. Your brother took a few slices of pizza for his friends. Then, there were 36 slices left. You decide to share the 36 slices evenly between you and your 8 friends. How many slices will each person get?

   A. 4

   B. 6

   C. 9

   D. 27

3. In a video game, you get 22 points every time you pass a street sign. How many signs do you have to pass to get 330 points?

   A. 12

   B. 15

   C. 18

   D. 20

4. You are making a game to play at your party. You plan to use a multiplication table to play the game you invented. You have to fill in the table and make copies for your friends. Fill in the table.

0	1	2	3	4	5	6	7	8	9	10
1										
2										
3										
4										
5										
6										
7										
8										
9										
10										

5. You have $65 to buy baseball cards. How many packs of baseball cards can you buy if each pack costs $5? Write your answer as a sentence.

Excellent Job!

Checking In

❶ Answers for pages 156 and 157:

1. D

2. A

3. B

4. An A+ answer: The multiplication table should be filled in correctly.

5. An A+ answer: "I can buy 13 packs of baseball cards."

Did your child answer the questions correctly? If so, review the questions with her to check what methods she used. For example, with question 5, explain that since the question asked how many packs could be bought from the money she had, the number of packs is the divisor. Then, give her another division question.

Did your child answer any of the questions incorrectly? If so, your kid might have trouble with multiplication. Work together to complete the table in question 5. If he has difficulty, remind him that he can skip-count by 2s, 3s, and so on. Let him know that this is the same as multiplying. Then, work together to review the division problems. You can have your kid use beans to work through the division problems. For example, with question 2, give your child 36 beans and then ask him to divide them up into 9 equal groups of beans.

Watch Out!

If your kid can't complete the table in question 5, let her know that she has to learn only half the table. Each number in the table has a "partner" that gives the same answer. Go over some rules and tips: Any number times 0 is 0; any number times 1 is that number; when multiplying by 9, the digits in the product always add up to 9: $9 \times 2 = 18$, $9 \times 3 = 27$, $9 \times 3 = 36$, and so on. Encourage your kid to find patterns. This will help her remember the facts. Remind your kid that division is the reverse of multiplication, so if she knows a multiplication fact, she also knows the division—for example, $3 \times 6 = 18$, and $18 \div 6 = 3$.

What to Know...

Multiplication and division are used a lot in real life. Your kid uses multiplication and division while making purchases and while playing all kinds of games. Your kid can work to master these skills by memorizing multiplication and division facts.

Review these skills with your child this way:

- **Equal groups** are groups that all have the same number of objects.
- **Multiplication** is an operation that combines equal groups to find a result.
- A **factor** is a number multiplied by another number.
- A **product** is a number that is the result of multiplying numbers.
- **Division** is an operation on two numbers that tells how many groups are in a number. Division also tells how many are in each group. The division sign is ÷.
- The **quotient** is a number resulting from dividing a number by another number. In 24 ÷ 3 = 8, the quotient is 8.
- The **dividend** is a number that is divided by another number. In 24 ÷ 3 = 8, the dividend is 24.
- The **divisor** is a number that another number is divided by. In 24 ÷ 3 = 8, the divisor is 3.

You and your child might find out how to manage a budget while shopping.

Skates $15   Stuffed Animals $5

Chess

Board Games $10

$120

Encourage your child to find out how many stuffed animals he can buy with $120. Then, do the same for board games and skates.

Your nature lover might want to find the distance a frog hops.

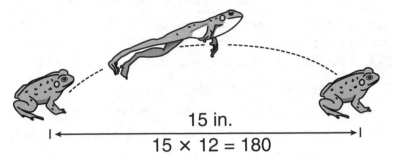

15 in.

15 × 12 = 180

Checking In

Ask your child to make sure the total distance the frog covers in 12 hops is correct.

Your child might run into trouble multiplying or dividing multi-digit numbers. Tell him that he can multiply by a two-digit number in different ways. For example, he can multiply the digit in the ones place of the first factor by the second factor, then the digit in the tens place of the first factor by the second factor. For example, when multiplying 15 × 12, he multiplies 5 by 12 (60), then 10 by 12 (120), and then adds the two products (60 + 120 = 180).

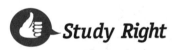

Study Right

The standard procedure for long division that is taught in school has a series of steps. Kids sometimes find them hard to remember. You can help your child remember these steps using the memory device **D**ead **M**onkeys **S**mell **B**ad **D**ad to remember to **D**ivide, **M**ultiply, **S**ubtract, **B**ring **D**own. Have your child repeat the steps out loud as he or she performs the long division.

On Your Way to an "A" Activities

$\left\{\begin{array}{c}\textbf{20}\\ \textbf{minutes}\end{array}\right\}$ Type: Game/Competitive
Materials needed: index cards, marker
Number of players: 2 or more

Play a game of "Concentration." Write multiplication and division facts on one set of cards, and their products and quotients on another set. Turn the question cards facedown on the right and the answer cards facedown on the left. Each player gets a chance to turn over a question card and an answer card. If they match, the player gets a point and goes again. If they don't match, the player turns the cards facedown again, and the next player gets a turn. The player with the most points at the end of the game wins.

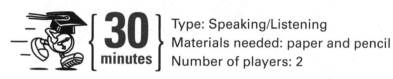

$\left\{\begin{array}{c}\textbf{30}\\ \textbf{minutes}\end{array}\right\}$ Type: Speaking/Listening
Materials needed: paper and pencil
Number of players: 2

Play "Rhythm Multiplication." Each player takes a turn to clap out a rhythm that is really a multiplication problem—a series of claps in equal sets. For example, if one player claps 3 sets of 6 claps. The next player writes the problem on paper ($3 \times 6 = 18$). If the writer does not get the correct problem, the clapper will write the correct problem, and the clapper will go again. If the problem is correct, switch roles.

Has your child breezed through the activities? If so, he or she can work on this Using Your Head activity independently.

Using Your Head

{ 20 } minutes

*Grab some **paper** and a **pencil**!*

You and 3 friends are going to see a movie. You put all your money together and you have $40. How many of each of these items will you and your friends buy, and how much will they cost?

$3　　　　$2　　　　$1　　　　$2　　　　$4

Do you have any money left over? How much?

Fractions and Decimals

Fourth graders have a pretty good understanding that a part of a pizza or a part of a chocolate bar is a fraction. Decimals are a whole other matter, but they are also used to show parts of a whole. So, if your kid has 10 colored pencils, and he grabs 5 of them, he may not realize that he can represent what he has in his hand as a decimal as well as a fraction. Up until now, he has probably worked on fractions and decimals separately, so it might be a bit of a challenge to bring these two concepts together.

Teachers expect kids to develop their skills with both fractions and decimals—using them in operations, finding equivalent decimals and fractions, using them in measurements, and so on. It's important for your child to understand the concepts of fractions and decimals, as well as the relationship between them. You need to provide him with visual models and a good bit of practice. This way he'll grab hold of the idea that he can use fractions and decimals to show the same amounts.

First things first: Get a sense of what your kid already knows. Turn the page and tell your kid to Jump Right In!

Here's what you'll need for this lesson:

- *paper*
- *pencil*
- *marker*
- *construction paper*
- *scissors*
- *ruler*
- *colored pencils*

Jodi bought a chocolate bar, shown below. Use this to answer questions 1 through 3.

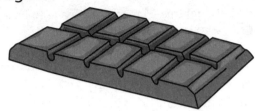

1. What if Jodi wants to save 3 pieces of her chocolate bar? Which fraction of her chocolate bar does she want to save?

   A. $\dfrac{1}{10}$ **C.** $\dfrac{1}{3}$

   B. $\dfrac{3}{10}$ **D.** $\dfrac{10}{3}$

2. What if Jodi's sister wants 2 pieces of the chocolate bar? What decimal shows this amount?

   A. 0.2

   B. 1.2

   C. 2.10

   D. 10.2

3. What if one-half of Jodi's chocolate bar melted? How many pieces out of the 10 pieces melted?

   A. 1

   B. 2

   C. 5

   D. 10

Tia and Brian are making bracelets with beads. For questions 4 through 5, write your answers as sentences.

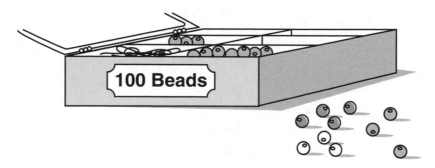

4. What fraction of the 100 beads are red?

5. What decimal shows how many beads are red?

6. There are 100 beads in the box, and 40 of them are red. Shade the grid below to represent the red beads.

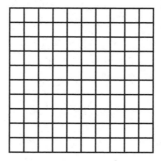

What fraction represents the shaded squares?

What decimal represents the shaded squares?

Excellent Job!

 **Checking In**

● Answers for pages 164 and 165:

1. B

2. A

3. C

4. An A+ answer: "$\frac{4}{10}$ of the beads are red."

5. An A+ answer: "0.4 of the beads are red."

6. An A+ answer. There should be 40 blocks shaded. $\frac{40}{100}$ represents the beads that are red. 0.40 represents the beads that are red.

If your child answered correctly, say, "Show me how you found the fraction $\frac{4}{10}$ for question 4" or "How did you find the decimal 0.2 for question 2?" Have your kid explain his understanding of the numbers to the right of the decimal.

If your child answered incorrectly, review each question. Ask, "What does the bottom number of a fraction show? What does the top number show?" Remind your kid that the **d**enominator of a fraction is *down* below the line and shows the total number of equal parts. She can remember that both **d**enominator and **d**own begin with **d**. Remind her that for decimals, **ten**ths is out of **ten** parts and **hundred**ths is out of one **hundred** parts. Your kid can use the mnemonic **TOoTH** to remind her of place value (**T**ens **O**nes **o T**enths **H**undredths), where the second **o** stands for the decimal. This will remind her that there are no ones after the decimal; it goes straight to tenths.

 **Watch Out!**

If your kid had a hard time with question 1, have him fold a strip of paper into equal parts and color the parts to represent the fraction. Or use manipulatives, like dried macaroni, beads, dried beans, etc. Do the same for questions about decimals. For example, for question 6, you can use 100 beans to represent the 100 beads, and then count out 40 beans to show 40 red beads and write $\frac{40}{100}$ or 0.40.

What to Know...

Your kid uses fractions and decimals in real life while making measurements and using money. With practice, your child will be able to continue to build on these skills and eventually master them.

Review these skills with your child this way:

- A **fraction** is a number that shows part of a group or part of a whole.

- A **numerator** is the number in a fraction that is above the line. The numerator tells how many parts of the whole are being counted.

- A **denominator** is the number in a fraction below the line. The denominator tells how many equal parts are in the whole.

- **Whole numbers** are numbers including zero and the counting numbers (0, 1, 2, 3, 4,...).

- A **mixed number** has a whole number and a fraction.

- A **decimal** is a number that has a decimal point. Decimals include values to the right of the decimal point that are part of a whole number.

- A **digit** is a symbol that is used to write numbers. There are 10 digits: 0, 1, 2, 3, 4, 5, 6, 7, 8, and 9.

- **Place value** is the value of a digit based on its place in a number. For example, in the number 382, the digit 8 is in the tens place, so it has a value of 80.

You and your child might use fractions and mixed numbers in a recipe.

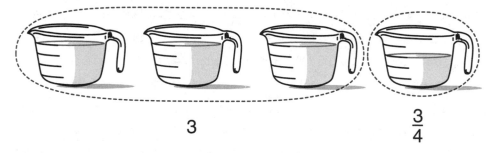

$$3 \qquad \frac{3}{4}$$

Each measuring cup is divided into 4 equal parts. Point out that 3 measuring cups are filled with flour and 1 measuring cup has 3 out of 4 fourths filled with flour.

Architects or construction workers might measure the plans on a miniature drawing.

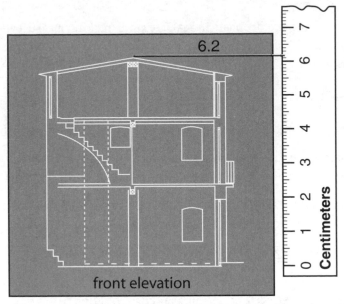

front elevation

Ask your child to use a centimeter ruler to measure her hand's dimensions. Then, have her draw out a construction plan for another hand that's the same size as hers, expressing the results in decimal numbers. Then, ask her to show these numbers as mixed numbers or fractions as well.

 Checking In

To help your child with fractions, write two boxes divided by a bar: $\frac{\square}{\square}$. Then, cut a paper circle into equal parts. Explain that the total number of equal parts goes in the denominator. Then, shade a number of parts and explain that the number of shaded parts goes in the numerator. Do the same for decimals by dividing a piece of paper into 10 parts to show tenths, or 100 parts to show hundredths. Relate fractions and decimals by writing the numbers shown for tenths and hundredths as fractions. Two parts out of 10 = 0.2 = $\frac{2}{10}$ = $\frac{20}{100}$. Throughout these activities, emphasize the idea of *equal parts*. Fractions and decimals rely on the fact that things get broken up equally. Help your kid understand that the whole concept of fractions doesn't work if the parts are unequal. This goes for decimals as well—a single thing is divided into 10 equal parts to show tenths, and 100 equal parts to show hundredths.

On Your Way to an "A" Activities

15 minutes

Type: Arts and Crafts
Materials needed: measuring cups, sugar, corn syrup, peanut butter, cereal, a baking dish
Number of players: 2 or more

Work with a parent to use a recipe to create cereal bars. Measure the following in $\frac{1}{4}$-cup measuring cups: $\frac{1}{2}$ cup sugar, $\frac{1}{4}$ cup brown sugar, $1\frac{1}{4}$ cups corn syrup, $1\frac{1}{2}$ cups peanut butter, and 6 cups cereal. First, figure out how many $\frac{1}{4}$ cups go into each measurement, and then have your parent microwave the sugar and corn syrup. Mix in the peanut butter and stir until it's smooth. Lastly, mix in the cereal. You'll need to pour this mixture into the baking dish and even it out. Then, cut into equal bars and refrigerate. Serve when solid.

15 minutes

Type: Arts and Crafts
Materials needed: paper and pencil
Number of players: 2

Create "Decimal Bars." Cut 10 rectangles from construction paper. Divide each of five rectangles into 10 equal parts. Shade a part of each rectangle, and write the decimal amount on the other side of the rectangle. Divide the other five rectangles into 100 equal parts. Shade a part of each rectangle and write the decimal amount on the other side of the rectangle. Then, figure out what fraction each of these decimal bars is equal to. You could start keeping a list of fractions and decimals that are the same amount.

Fourth Graders Are...

Fourth graders are often interested in cooking and measuring things. They can gain experience with fractions and decimals in recipes, or building things that require measurements, like scale models. Regular practice using these skills helps tremendously.

Has your child breezed through the activities? If so, he or she can work on this Using Your Head activity independently.

Using Your Head

*Grab some **paper** and a **pencil**!*

Color amounts on the measuring cups to show a fraction and a decimal. Color the first cup to show an amount that represents $\frac{1}{2}$. Color the second cup to show an amount that represents 0.5.

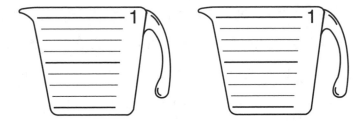

Draw your own cups and divide them into equal parts. Color in amounts and write the fraction or decimal amounts you colored.

Equivalent Fractions

Though it may take some practice, most fourth graders get the idea that fractions are parts of a whole. The next step will be to grab hold of the concept of equivalent fractions.

The subject is taught so quickly in the classroom that many kids don't fully understand all they need to. For one, the term *equivalent* is new to most fourth graders, and it is pretty abstract. It doesn't help that they rarely use equivalent fractions in the real world, with the exception of using and naming coins as a part of a dollar. But it's important for kids to develop a good understanding of equivalent fractions for the classroom.

To help your child fully understand the idea of equivalent fractions, take the opportunity to have him change the fractions he uses in his everyday life to equivalent fractions. You can also use coins, games, and arts and crafts to reinforce how to use equivalent fractions.

First things first: Get a sense of what your kid already knows. Turn the page and tell your kid to Jump Right In!

Here's what you'll need for this lesson:

- paper
- pencil
- marker
- change (dimes, quarters, and nickels)
- index cards
- construction paper
- felt
- scissors
- crayons
- glue

Jump Right In!

Kim baked 5 chocolate cupcakes and 3 marbled cupcakes.

1. $\frac{5}{8}$ of Kim's cupcakes are chocolate. What other fraction can Kim use to show the portion of cupcakes that are chocolate?

   A. $\frac{1}{8}$

   B. $\frac{2}{16}$

   C. $\frac{10}{16}$

   D. $\frac{10}{8}$

2. Kim put strawberry frosting on 2 of her 8 cupcakes. What other fraction can Kim use to show that $\frac{2}{8}$ of the cupcakes have frosting?

   A. $\frac{1}{8}$

   B. $\frac{1}{4}$

   C. $\frac{1}{2}$

   D. $\frac{4}{8}$

Michael took 12 shots during his basketball game. Use this information to answer questions 3 and 4 in full sentences.

3. Michael made 6 baskets. Write a fraction to show the baskets Michael made out of the number of shots he took. Then, write two more fractions that show this same amount.

4. What is the relationship between the numerator and denominator in each fraction that you've written?

Excellent Job!

 *Checking In*

ⓐAnswers for pages 172 and 173:

1. C

2. B

3. An A+ answer: "Michael made $\frac{6}{12}$ of the baskets. Examples of other fractions that show the same amount are $\frac{1}{2}$ and $\frac{12}{24}$."

4. An A+ answer. "Each denominator is two times the numerator."

If your child answered correctly, ask, "How did you find the equivalent fraction?" Have your kid show you how she figured out the answer.

If your child answered incorrectly, review each question. Show your child that **equi**valent and **equ**al both begin with the same letters, so he can think of something equivalent as being equal. Ask, "How do you find a fraction with the same value as another fraction?" Help your child to multiply (or divide) the numerator and denominator by the same number to get an equivalent fraction.

 *Watch Out!*

Your kid might have a hard time understanding why two fractions are equivalent. In examples 1 through 3, she may have chosen a fraction with the same denominator as the fraction in the question. Help her understand equivalent fractions by folding a piece of paper in two equal parts. Then, have her color one part, and use a fraction to show the colored part. Then, fold the same paper into four equal parts, and have her write a fraction for the colored part. Explain that the same amount is colored, but now there are four equal parts and two are colored. Then, fold the paper into eighths. Repeat this process with thirds and sixths.

What to Know...

Finding equivalence is a necessary skill for all kinds of people in the world, from butchers to architects to cashiers and pharmacists. Kids need practice with equivalent fractions because they will have to build on these skills later in order to add and subtract unlike fractions. To work with equivalent fractions, your child needs to understand the terms *numerator* and *denominator* (be sure to review these definitions on page 167).

Review these skills with your child this way:

- A **fraction** is a number that shows part of a group or part of a whole.
- A **factor** is a number multiplied by another number.

A cashier will need to know equivalent fractions to show a part of a dollar to make change.

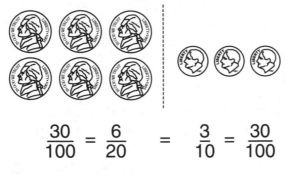

$$\frac{30}{100} = \frac{6}{20} = \frac{3}{10} = \frac{30}{100}$$

Ask your child to use different amounts of change to represent a part of a dollar. Show him or her that 2 quarters and 5 dimes are the same amount. Both are $\frac{5}{10}$ or $\frac{1}{2}$ of a dollar. Have your kid come up with other equivalent fractions using dimes, quarters, and nickels.

 *Checking In*

If your kid gets stuck, show him how to make equivalent fractions by multiplying the numerator and denominator of one fraction by the same number, or factor, in order to find an equivalent fraction. For example, $\frac{4}{5} \times \frac{2}{2} = \frac{8}{10}$. Be sure that your kid understands what *equivalent* means. Equivalent fractions are fractions that are composed of different numbers, but they show the same part of a whole. Once your kid understands this concept, give him a fraction like $\frac{3}{9}$ and have him multiply the numerator and denominator by 2 to get an equivalent fraction. Or give him a fraction like $\frac{18}{45}$ and have him divide the numerator and denominator by 9.

On Your Way to an "A" Activities

30 minutes

Type: Arts and Crafts
Materials needed: felt (in two different colors), scissors, glue, marker
Number of players: 2 or more

Create "Equivalent Dominoes." Each player cuts out rectangles to make dominoes and uses a ruler to divide the rectangles into two parts. One player creates a domino by gluing felt dots (in a different color from the rectangle) on the top part and then on the bottom part of the domino. The other player creates a domino that is *equivalent* to the first player's domino by multiplying (or dividing) the number of dots on the top and bottom parts by the same number. Each player takes turns making the first domino for the second player to follow with the *equivalent*.

10 minutes

Type: Active
Materials needed: two identical measuring cups with fractional measurements on the side
Number of players: 2 or more—you and a parent or friend

Play "Follow the Leader" for equivalent fractions. Place a certain amount of water in a measuring cup and call out the fraction amount, such as "one-half." The other player must place the same amount of water in his or her measuring cup and call out a fraction that is equivalent (but has a different name), such as "two-fourths." Each person takes a turn going first.

Fourth Graders Are...

Fourth graders are often interested in playing games and doing arts and crafts. Offer opportunities for regular practice to play games and do arts and crafts that involve equivalent fractions.

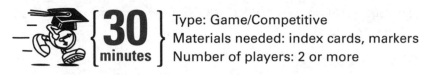

Type: Game/Competitive
Materials needed: index cards, markers
Number of players: 2 or more

Play a game of "Fishing for Equivalence." Each player writes a different fraction on each of 10 index cards. Then, each player writes an equivalent fraction for each of these 10 fractions on 10 other index cards. Put all the cards together, shuffle them, and give 5 cards to each player. The rest of the cards remain in a pile. Each player matches the equivalent fractions they have and places them aside. Then, the first player asks the next player for a card that is equivalent to a fraction in his or her hand. If the player has one, he or she will give it to the player who asked. If the player does not have one, the player who asked will take a card from the pile, and the next player gets a turn to ask for an equivalent fraction card. The game continues until all the matches are made. The player with the most sets of equivalent fractions wins the game.

Has your child breezed through the activities? If so, he or she can work on this Using Your Head activity independently.

Using Your Head

*Grab some **crayons** and a **pencil**!*

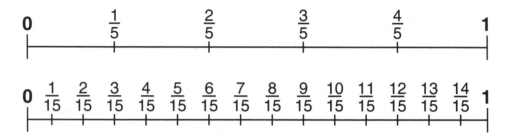

1. Shade an amount on both number lines to show $\frac{1}{5}$.

2. Now, write an equivalent fraction for $\frac{1}{5}$ with a denominator of 15.

3. Now, draw a number line below divided into 20 equal parts, and write an equivalent fraction for $\frac{1}{5}$ with a denominator of 20.

Answer: 1. 1/5, 3/15 shaded; 2. 3/15; 3. 4/20

Adding and Subtracting Fractions

Adding and subtracting fractions is confusing for some middle-school students, so imagine how difficult it must be for fourth graders who are doing it for the first time. Adding and subtracting fractions is different from regular addition and subtraction, which can further contribute to your kid's confusion.

At home, children hardly ever need to add or subtract fractions, so they really don't practice this concept much, except in the classroom. As kids get older, they may need to add and subtract fractions in the real world—especially for measurements. In the classroom, fourth graders are expected to add and subtract fractions with like and unlike denominators. It's important for kids to learn how to do this since they will continue to add and subtract fractions in every area of math.

To help your child fully understand how to add and subtract fractions, you can use models. You can also apply these skills to areas that your children enjoy, such as sports, games, cooking, and so on.

First things first: Get a sense of what your kid already knows. Turn the page and tell your kid to Jump Right In!

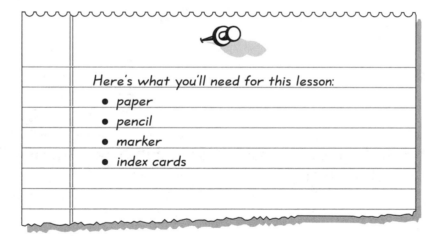

Here's what you'll need for this lesson:
- *paper*
- *pencil*
- *marker*
- *index cards*

Jump Right In!

Raheem is making trail mix. Use the pictures below to answer questions 1 through 3.

$$\frac{2}{8} \qquad\qquad \frac{4}{8} \qquad\qquad \frac{1}{2}$$

1. If Raheem mixes the pretzels and raisins, how much will he have altogether?

   A. $\frac{3}{8}$ C. $\frac{6}{8}$

   B. $\frac{6}{16}$ D. $\frac{7}{8}$

2. If Raheem mixes the raisins and goldfish, how much will he have altogether?

   A. $\frac{1}{6}$ C. $\frac{4}{8}$

   B. $\frac{3}{10}$ D. $\frac{3}{4}$

3. If Raheem eats $\frac{1}{8}$ of a cup of the pretzels, how much will he have left?

A. $\frac{1}{3}$

C. $\frac{1}{2}$

B. $\frac{3}{8}$

D. $\frac{3}{4}$

4. Raheem poured $\frac{1}{2}$ cup of juice into a glass. Then, he spilled $\frac{3}{8}$ of a cup of juice out of the glass he poured. Use the number line to subtract $\frac{3}{8}$ from $\frac{1}{2}$. Then, write the difference.

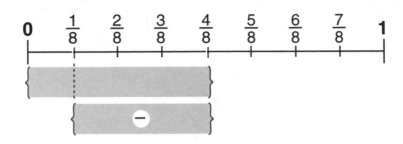

5. A chef mixed $\frac{1}{8}$ cup of milk with $\frac{3}{8}$ cup of water. Use the number line to add $\frac{1}{8}$ and $\frac{3}{8}$. Then, write the sum.

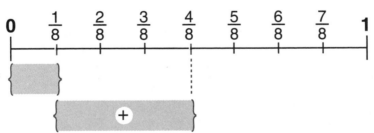

Excellent Job!

 **Checking In**

Ⓐ Answers for pages 180 through 182:

1. C

2. D

3. B

4. An A+ answer: "$\frac{1}{2} - \frac{3}{8} = \frac{1}{8}$."

5. An A+ answer: "$\frac{1}{8} + \frac{3}{8} = \frac{4}{8}$ or $\frac{1}{2}$."

If your child answered correctly, ask, "What did you do to find the answer?" Have your kid walk you through the steps she took.

If your kid answered incorrectly, review each question. Ask, "What do you do when you add or subtract fractions with like (or unlike) denominators?" Remind your child that to add or subtract unlike fractions, he has to turn them into like fractions by finding equivalent fractions. For example, in question 4, the fractions are unlike fractions. Remind him that denominators are the numbers below the dividing line, and to be **eq**uivalent they have to be **eq**ual in both fractions before they can be added or subtracted. To do this, your kid can multiply both the numerator and denominator of $\frac{1}{2}$ by 4.

 **Watch Out!**

Some kids don't realize that they should add or subtract only the numerators when they're adding and subtracting like fractions. So they add the numerators together as well as the denominators. To help your child with this problem, have her color fraction strips from rectangles that are the same size. Then, have her place the strips next to each other. You can then use a third rectangle that she can color in to show the addition or subtraction. In order to correctly add or subtract fractions, they have to have the same denominator, or number of parts in the whole. Show her that when fractions are added or subtracted, only the numerator, or the number of colored parts, will change. When using like fractions, the number of parts in the denominator always remains the same.

What to Know...

Your child needs to understand the terms *fraction*, *numerator*, and *denominator* (review these definitions on page 167) before moving on to these new skills.

Review these skills with your child this way:

- A **multiple** is a number that is a product of a whole number and another number. For example, 5 × 2 = 10, so 10 is a multiple of 5. The numbers 15, 20, and 25 are all multiples of 5.

- The **greatest common factor (GCF)** is the greatest of the factors that are shared by two numbers.

- The **least common denominator (LCD)** is the lowest multiple that is shared by the denominators of two or more fractions.

Your child can add and subtract fractions, such as measurements.

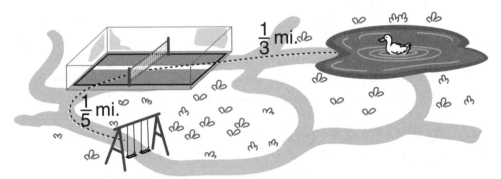

$$\frac{1}{5} \text{ mi.} + \frac{1}{3} \text{ mi.} = \frac{8}{15} \text{ mi.}$$

 *Checking In*

Ask your child how far you would walk from the swings to the pond.

To find a common denominator for these fractions, your kid should list multiples of 5 (5, 10, 15, 20, and so on) and multiples of 3 (3, 6, 9, 12, 15, 18, and so on). Then, he should pick the first multiple that matches (15). This is the Least Common Denominator. Now, your kid needs to identify what factor multiplied with 5 results in 15 (3), and then multiply the numerator and denominator in $\frac{1}{5}$, by 3. For $\frac{1}{5}$ he would multiply by 3 to get $\frac{3}{15}$, and for $\frac{1}{3}$ he would multiply by 5 to get $\frac{5}{15}$. From here he would be able to add the numerators and solve the problem. Reinforce the fact that if the denominators are the same, the numerators are just added or subtracted; if they're different, then the fractions must be changed to equivalent fractions.

On Your Way to an "A" Activities

{ 10 minutes } Type: Reading/Writing
Materials needed: a paper pizza and pencil
Number of players: 1 or more

Add with a "Fraction Pizza." Draw a pizza on paper and then cut it into equal slices. Remove some of the pizza and write a fraction that shows the amount you have taken away from the whole pizza. Then, remove another part of the pizza and write a fraction to show that amount. Add the two amounts. Write down the fraction of the pizza that is left after you remove the two amounts. Finally, replace the slices to make it whole again.

{ 45 minutes } Type: Game/Competitive
Materials needed: index cards, markers
Number of players: 2 or more

Play a game of "Fraction Bingo." Make bingo cards by making a 5-by-5 grid on an index card. In each square, write a different fraction amount (except in 2 squares write FREE). On separate cards, write addition or subtraction questions with different fractions as the correct answer. Make sure that each fraction on the bingo cards has a corresponding question card. The "caller" will keep the question cards and call out an addition or subtraction question. The players will mark their cards for each fraction that is an answer. The first player to fill a row (vertically, horizontally, or diagonally) wins.

Fourth Graders Are...

Fourth graders love to play games and measure things. Don't hesitate to integrate the skills you are working on with them into the games that you play together. Recipes are always a good way for kids to visualize adding fractions.

Has your child breezed through the activities? If so, he or she can work on this Using Your Head activity independently.

Using Your Head

{ **20** }
minutes

*Grab a **pencil**!*

Raheem, Miranda, and Terry are on a picnic.

1. If Raheem brought 1 cup of his trail mix and they ate $\frac{1}{4}$ cup of it, how much trail mix is left?

2. If Terry brought $\frac{1}{3}$ of a loaf of bread and Miranda brought $\frac{1}{2}$ of a loaf of bread, how much bread do they have altogether?

3. Birds ate another $\frac{3}{8}$ of a cup of Raheem's trail mix. Use your answer to question 1 to figure out how much trail mix they have left.

Answers: 1. $\frac{3}{4}$ of a cup of trail mix; 2. $\frac{5}{6}$ of a loaf of bread; 3. $\frac{3}{8}$ of a cup of trail mix

Adding and Subtracting Decimals

Fourth graders usually see decimals only with money values. They see decimals on the price of store items, on receipts, and so on. They may even have to add decimal values when buying things, or subtract decimal values when trying to make change.

Because this is one of the only places kids see decimals, a lot of them still have limited knowledge of the concept of place value. The best way to help your kid understand addition and subtraction with decimals is to extend the place value system (hundreds, tens, ones, and so on) so that it includes the place values to the right of the decimal. Once she understands that decimals are similar to whole numbers, she will have an easier time adding and subtracting decimals.

To help your child build these skills, use real-life situations that he is familiar with—such as adding and subtracting decimals with money, measurements, scores (as in gymnastics or figure skating), and so on. With a little practice, your child can soon master adding and subtracting decimals.

First things first: Get a sense of what your kid already knows. Turn the page and tell your kid to Jump Right In!

Here's what you'll need for this lesson:
- *paper*
- *markers or crayons*
- *pencils*
- *construction paper*
- *game piece*
- *poster board*

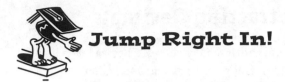

Checkerboard Cafe

Pizza Slice....$2.50

Hamburger....$2.25

Onion Rings..$1.25

French Fries..$0.75

Soda $0.90

Juice $1.25

Cookie $0.50

1. Julia bought a hamburger and a soda. How much did Julia pay?

    A. $2.15

    B. $3.15

    C. $11.25

    D. $21.15

2. Kari had $4.58. She bought a bottle of juice for $1.25. How much did Kari have left?

    A. $2.33

    B. $3.23

    C. $3.32

    D. $3.33

3. Steve had $5.00. He bought a slice of pizza and a juice. How much change did Steve receive?

    A. $0.75

    B. $2.10

    C. $1.25

    D. $1.30

Steve and Kari are planning to ride in a bike-a-thon this weekend. Write your answers for questions 4 and 5 as sentences.

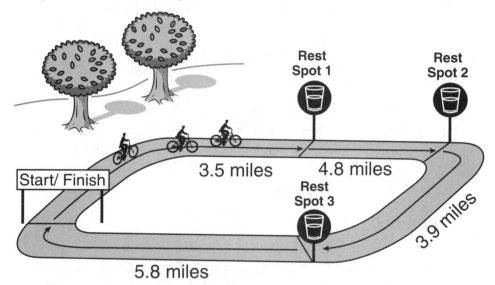

4. Steve and Kari rode from the "Start" to "Rest Spot 1" and then to "Rest Spot 2." How far did they ride in all?

5. The riders in the bike-a-thon had to ride a total of 18 miles. The second-place rider had 3.2 miles to go when the winner crossed the finish line. How far had the second-place rider gone when the winner crossed the finish line?

Excellent Job!

 *Checking In*

ⒶAnswers for pages 188 and 189:

1. B

2. D

3. C

4. An A+ answer: "Steve and Kari rode 8.3 miles."

5. An A+ answer: "The second-place rider had ridden 14.8 miles."

Did your child get the correct answers? If so, ask, "How did you figure out how far Steve and Kari rode?" Have your kid walk you through his work. Make sure he knew the skills (and didn't guess).

Did your child get one of the answers wrong? If so, go over the incorrect answers together. For question 3, ask, "How did you figure out the amount of change Steve received?" For question 5, ask, "What numbers did you use to figure out how far the second-place rider had ridden?"

 Watch Out!

Sometimes the decimal point throws fourth graders off when adding and subtracting. Draw a chart like the one below to help your kid put the digits in the correct place value. Then, have him or her write the numbers from one of the problems in the chart. Make sure your child understands that the numbers to the right of the decimal are added and subtracted the same way as the numbers to the left of the decimal.

Tens	Ones	.	Tenths	Hundredths

What to Know...

Kids are going to have to get used to adding and subtracting decimals on an everyday basis as they get older. Further study in math and the sciences will require this, as well as any purchases they make—from going to the movies with friends to trips to the corner store.

Review these skills with your child this way:

- A **decimal** is a number that has a decimal point. Decimals include values to the right of the decimal point that are part of a whole number.

- A **decimal point** is the period in decimals that separates the tenths place and the ones place.

- A **digit** is a symbol that is used to write numbers. There are 10 digits: 0, 1, 2, 3, 4, 5, 6, 7, 8, and 9.

- **Place value** is the value of a digit based on its place in a number. For example, in the number 382, the digit 8 is in the tens place, so it has a value of 80.

Your child could also add distances when he is traveling to a relative's or friend's house.

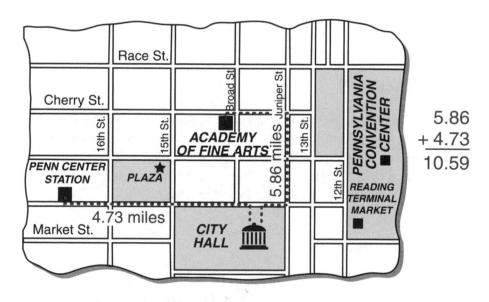

$$\begin{array}{r} 5.86 \\ + 4.73 \\ \hline 10.59 \end{array}$$

Encourage your child to add distances or lengths with decimals.

Your child might add the prices of items when you go shopping and subtract to find the change received.

25.00
−19.50
5.50

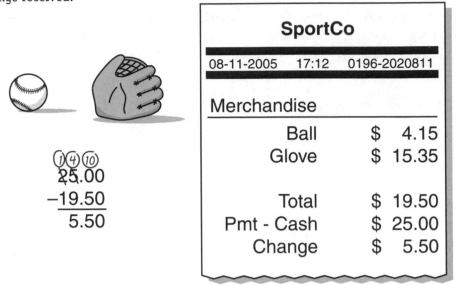

SportCo

08-11-2005   17:12   0196-2020811

Merchandise

Ball	$ 4.15
Glove	$ 15.35
Total	$ 19.50
Pmt - Cash	$ 25.00
Change	$ 5.50

Ask your child to add the cost of the ball and the glove. Remind her that she may have to regroup (for example, 5 ones + 5 ones = 10 ones, or 1 ten and 0 ones). Then, ask her to subtract to find the change. Again, remind her to regroup when needed (for example, to subtract 5 tenths from 0 tenths, she should regroup 1 one as 10 tenths and rewrite the 5 in the ones place and the 0 in the tenths place of $25.00 to show 4 ones and 10 tenths).

👉 Checking In

If your child is having a hard time, you may want to use models. When working with decimals to the tenths place, draw rectangles divided into ten equal parts. When working with decimals to the hundredths place, draw a 10-by-10 grid. Have your child color the models to show a given amount. Then, your kid can add or subtract the amounts in the models by coloring in more to add or crossing off to subtract.

👍 Study Right

When adding and subtracting decimals, your child should always mark whenever she regroups. Kids tend to want to skip steps as certain procedures become more automatic. But marking when she regroups will help her keep track of what numbers to use and will prevent careless errors. For example, when regrouping 1 one into 10 tenths in the example above, your child should draw a line through the 5 in the ones place and write a 4 above it, and then draw a line through the 0 in the tenths place and write a 10 above it.

On Your Way to an "A" Activities

{20 minutes}

Type: Game/Competitive
Materials needed: construction paper, marker, game piece
Number of players: 2 or more

Play "Decimal Football." Make a game board by cutting the construction paper into a rectangular football field and drawing 10 equal lines and two end zones. Place a game piece on a line in the middle of the field. Decide which player goes first. The second player gives the first player an addition or subtraction question with decimals. If the first player gets the correct answer, he advances one line on the field toward the next player's end zone. The first player continues to advance as long as he gives the correct answers. If the first player misses, the second player gets a chance to answer questions, moving the game piece in the opposite direction. The player who scores the most wins.

{20 minutes}

Type: Reading/Writing
Materials needed: newspaper, paper, pencil, poster board, markers
Number of players: 1 or more

Get a newspaper or watch a weather channel to find the amount of precipitation (rain or snow) in your area. Add the amount of rainfall each day to get a total for one week. Then, find the amount of rainfall for the next week. Find the difference between the rainfall for the two weeks. Make a poster to show your results. You can add to your poster each week. Make your poster interesting by using symbols, colors, and other things to help keep track of the amounts. Try to predict the amount of precipitation that you will get each day or each week.

Has your child breezed through the activities? If so, he or she can work on this Using Your Head activity independently.

Using Your Head

{ 25 minutes }

*Grab a **pencil**!*

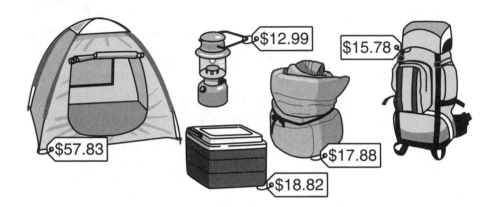

$12.99 $15.78 $57.83 $17.88 $18.82

You need to buy as many items as you can to go camping, but you have only $75.00 to spend. List two different sets of items you could buy using only $75.00.

<u>Set A</u>   <u>Set B</u>

If you purchased Set A, how much money would you have left? Set B?

Answers: Possible sets—Tent and backpack with $1.39 left over; sleeping bag, lantern, cooler, and backpack with $9.53 left over

Two- and Three-Dimensional Shapes

Your fourth grader is expected to know the names of many different shapes and be able to tell the difference between a two- and a three-dimensional shape. There are two- and three-dimensional shapes everywhere we go. Kids learn shapes early on, but they often overgeneralize. They may be encouraged to describe a ball as a circle (which is two-dimensional) when it's technically a sphere (a three-dimensional shape). Some kids are confused by three-dimensional shapes because they see two-dimensional shapes on the faces of three-dimensional shapes, like a rectangle on the face of a box. Then, they may think the box itself is two-dimensional.

One way to distinguish between two- and three-dimensional shapes is to give your kids these simple definitions. Two-dimensional shapes cannot carry anything inside of them because they're flat and they don't have any depth. Three-dimensional shapes do have depth and can carry stuff inside of them. Your kid will often see three-dimensional shapes represented on a piece of paper, which is not three-dimensional, and this can be tricky. You can help him distinguish between two- and three-dimensional shapes by having him handle three-dimensional objects and by showing him how these shapes might look on a two-dimensional piece of paper.

First things first: Get a sense of what your kid already knows. Turn the page and tell your kid to Jump Right In!

Here's what you'll need for this lesson:
- boxes
- construction paper
- scissors
- glue
- tape
- modeling clay
- toothpicks
- pipe cleaners
- sparkles
- timer

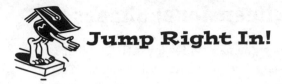

Jump Right In!

On his way to school, Carlos saw a lot of different street signs.

1. This sign was next to the railroad tracks.

What shape is the sign?

A. circle

B. rectangle

C. square

D. triangle

2. This sign tells people how fast they can drive.

What shape is the sign?

A. hexagon

B. rectangle

C. square

D. triangle

3. Before Carlos crossed the street, he saw this sign.

What shape is the sign?

A. circle

B. pentagon

C. hexagon

D. octagon

4. Tina was helping her neighbor gather items for a yard sale. Tina found the items shown in the picture below. Name the shape of each item.

_____ _____ _____ _____ _____ _____

5. Kamal drew the house in the picture below.

Name each three-dimensional shape that you see in the picture and circle the two-dimensional shapes that you see in the picture.

Excellent Job!

 *Checking In*

Ⓐ Answers for pages 196 and 197:

1. A

2. B

3. D

4. An A+ answer: Students should write each of the following: Under the basketball, "sphere"; under the party hat, "cone"; under the doorstop, "triangular prism"; under the paint can, "cylinder"; under the box, "cube"; and under the wooden box, "rectangular prism."

5. An A+ answer: Students should write "cylinder." Students should circle all *circles, squares,* and *rectangles* in the picture.

Did your child get the correct answers? If so, ask, "How did you know the names of all of those shapes?" Encourage your kid to tell you stories about shapes and when he first remembers knowing the names of them. You could even ask where he started learning the names.

Did your child get one of the answers wrong? If your child answered questions 1, 2, or 3 incorrectly, she might not know the characteristics of different two-dimensional shapes. Go over the incorrect answers. Ask, "How many sides does that shape have?" Point out that a **tri**angle has three sides just as a **tri**cycle has three wheels. Point out that any flat shape with more than four straight sides has -**gon** at the end of its name because these are also poly**gon**s. Then, teach your child the prefixes **penta** for five, **hexa** for six, and **octa** for eight. This will help to build a strong foundation for her future understanding of geometry.

 *Watch Out!*

If your kid has trouble distinguishing between two- and three-dimensional shapes, find an old shoe box. Have your child explore the box. Explain that this is a three-dimensional shape made up of two-dimensional shapes. Take the box apart and show the different rectangles. Repeat this process for cylinders with a can and a paper-towel roll. Explain the circles on either end of the cylinders, and cut open the paper-towel roll so that the child can see that this part of the cylinder is simply a rectangle when it is opened up. Repeat the procedure for other three-dimensional objects you find around the home.

What to Know...

Your kid sees shapes everywhere he goes. The whole world is made up of shapes. He can identify shapes as he goes about his daily activities.

Review two-dimensional figures with your child this way:

- A **two-dimensional figure** has length and width.
- A **closed figure** is a two-dimensional figure in which all the sides connect and there is no opening.
- An **open figure** is a two-dimensional figure in which there is an opening because not all the lines connect.
- A **polygon** is a closed two-dimensional figure with straight sides.
- An **angle** is a figure formed by two lines that meet at a point.

Circle	Triangle	Rectangle
round with no straight sides	three straight sides, three angles	four straight angles, four straight sides, opposite sides equal
Pentagon	Hexagon	Octagon
five angles, five straight sides	six angles, six straight sides	eight angles, eight straight sides

 Checking In

If your child is having difficulty naming shapes, get a piece of wood and place nails in the wood in a five-by-five array so that the heads of the nails are exposed. Have her use rubber bands to create different two-dimensional shapes as you name them. After each shape, talk about the characteristics of the shape—number of sides, number of equal sides, square corners, and so on. Make sure your kid understands that a shape, such as a triangle, for example, can have equal sides or not, or have a square corner or not. Encourage her to try to create different types of triangles.

Review three-dimensional figures with your child this way:

- A **three-dimensional figure** has length, width, and height.
- A **face** is a flat side of a three-dimensional figure.

Your child can identify two- and three-dimensional shapes on the playground.

Sphere	Cone	Cube
no straight sides, like a ball	one face is a circle, like an ice cream cone	six faces, all the same-size squares
Cylinder	**Triangular prism**	**Rectangular prism**
two faces that are circles, like a can of beans	five faces, two are triangles of the same size and three are rectangles	six faces, all rectangles

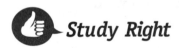 *Study Right*

Help your kid understand the relationship between a shape and its name. A pyramid is like the pyramids in Egypt with four triangular faces and one rectangular face. Use a sugar cube to show the six square faces that make up a cube. Make sure your kid understands the relationship between the name and the shape. Have your kid look at the shapes of the faces of three-dimensional shapes to name them. Encourage him to draw both two- and three-dimensional shapes, and have him keep a log of shapes that he is familiar with.

On Your Way to an "A" Activities

15 minutes

Type: Arts and Crafts
Materials needed: construction paper, scissors, glue, marker, sparkles
Number of players: 2 or more

Make a "Shape Collage." Cut different shapes from construction paper. Write the name of the shape on a separate piece of paper. Then, glue the shapes to a large sheet of construction paper to make a collage. Decorate your collage as you wish. Then, point out all of the shapes you've used to the other player.

20 minutes

Type: Reading/Writing
Materials needed: large cardboard boxes, timer
Number of players: 2 or more

Play "Shape Hunt." Each player will have two large cardboard boxes—one marked *two-dimensional shapes*, the other marked *three-dimensional shapes*. Set the timer for 10 minutes. Each player will gather and place two- and three-dimensional shapes in the appropriate box. After 10 minutes is up, each player names the shapes in each box. Two points are given for having and naming each two-dimensional object, and one point is given for having and naming each three-dimensional object. The player with the most points wins the game.

Has your child breezed through the activities? If so, he or she can work on this Using Your Head activity independently.

Using Your Head

Grab a **box**, some **construction paper**, **scissors**, **glue**, **modeling clay**, **toothpicks**, **pipe cleaners**, **tape**, and **sparkles**!

Use the materials to create a scene, or diorama, inside the box. The scene can be from a classroom, a house, an outdoor place, or a book you may have read. Use as many different kinds of shapes as you can—both two- and three-dimensional shapes.

In the space below, draw and name some of the shapes in your scene.

Symmetry

Kids see symmetry everywhere. There is symmetry in nature—in people, butterflies, leaves, and cats. Your child sees symmetry each time he or she looks in the mirror. There is symmetry in letters of the alphabet, in flags, and in shapes all around us.

Although fourth graders see symmetrical things everywhere, the term *symmetry* might be new and abstract. Teachers expect kids to know how to draw lines of symmetry in objects and shapes in the classroom. Presenting symmetry as a mirror image or a matching half will help your child better understand the concept of symmetry.

To help your kid build skills in recognizing and identifying symmetry, you can start with objects around the house. You can also use the two-dimensional shapes with which he or she is already familiar.

First things first: Get a sense of what your kid already knows. Turn the page and tell your kid to Jump Right In!

Here's what you'll need for this lesson:
- *tissue paper*
- *glue*
- *paper*
- *pencil*
- *white poster board*
- *ruler*
- *scissors*
- *crayons*

Jump Right In!

A group of friends went to the movies. Use the movie sign below to answer questions 1 through 3.

1. The letters below are on the sign. Which letter is <u>not</u> symmetrical?

    A E M R

    A. A

    B. E

    C. M

    D. R

2. The letter **I** is in the word MOVIE. How many lines of symmetry does the letter **I** have?

    A. 0

    B. 1

    C. 2

    D. 4

3. The movie sign is a rectangle. Which of these shows the correct line(s) of symmetry for a rectangle?

A.

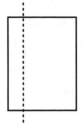

B.

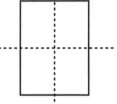

C.

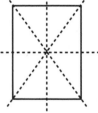

D.

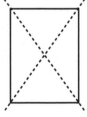

Some of the designs on the state flags of the United States have lines of symmetry. Answer questions 4 and 5 by completing the flags. To complete the flags, draw the other half of each flag using the line of symmetry shown in the drawings.

4.

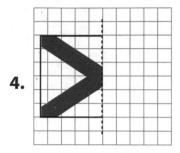

This is the flag for the state of Alabama.

5.

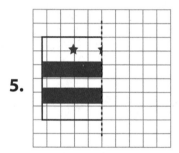

This is the flag for the District of Columbia.

Excellent Job!

 **Checking In**

A Answers for pages 204 through 206:

1. D

2. C

3. B

4. An A+ answer: A completed and symmetrical flag of the state of Alabama showing two lines crossing in the middle

5. An A+ answer: A completed and symmetrical flag of the District of Columbia

Did your child get the correct answers? If your kid really seems to understand symmetry, then give him a chance to show off his skills. Ask him to name 10 things in the room that are symmetrical as fast as he can. Then, have him name 10 things that aren't symmetrical.

Did your kid get one of the answers wrong? If so, go over the incorrect answers. Ask, "Does one part of the shape look exactly like the other part?" Have your child fold the paper so that one part of a shape falls on top of the other. If both parts line up exactly, then this is a line of symmetry. Do this with a variety of shapes to help your kid get the idea.

 **Watch Out!**

Some kids have trouble understanding symmetry. To help your child better understand this idea, use graph paper to draw half of a symmetrical shape or design, and then use a dotted line to show the line of symmetry. Have your kid draw the other half of the shape. Encourage her to fold the paper along the line to make sure the two halves are identical.

What to Know...

Kids can identify symmetry as they play in the park or the woods or at a playground. Your child can identify symmetry on signs he or she sees and even in people.

Review this skill with your child this way:

- The **line of symmetry** is the fold line for symmetry. If you folded a shape along its line of symmetry, then the two halves would match up. Shapes can have more than one line of symmetry.

Your child can identify lines of symmetry in nature.

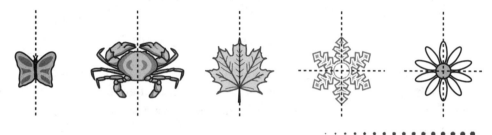

 **Checking In**

Go outdoors with your child. Help him or her find objects with symmetry. Have your child identify the lines of symmetry.

Have your kid check things out in your house to see if they're symmetrical. He could use a small mirror to divide the things he's looking at and to see if the object splits in any symmetrical ways. Or have him draw objects with multiple lines of symmetry and use the mirror to double-check his drawings. Make sure your kid is using straight lines to divide the shapes he's dealing with.

Fourth Graders Are...

Fourth graders like to use things they can touch and feel when they do math. You can have your kid place a mirror on the line of symmetry to see the other half of an object. If the reflection is the same as the other part of the object, then the line on which the mirror is placed is a line of symmetry.

On Your Way to an "A" Activities

15 minutes

Type: Arts and Crafts
Materials needed: paper, scissors, glue, pencil
Number of players: 1 or more

Make "Mirror Designs." Cut a square out of paper. Fold the square in half to form a rectangle or diagonally to form a triangle. Draw a design on one side of the paper (this will be half of a whole design). Cut out the design you drew. Open up the paper and press flat. Fold another square into a rectangle, then fold it over again and draw something. This object will have two lines of symmetry. You can mount the designs on paper of a contrasting color.

15 minutes

Type: Reading/Writing
Materials needed: paper, pencil, crayons
Number of players: 2 or more

Play "I'm Copying You!" Draw a line down the center of a piece of paper. One player will begin at the line and draw on one side of the line. The other player will draw a mirror image on the other side of the line. Each player will take turns going first until a symmetrical picture is formed. (You can draw or color parts when you go first.) When the picture is complete, fold the paper along the line to make sure the two parts are mirror images.

Has your child breezed through the activities? If so, he or she can work on this Using Your Head activity independently.

Using Your Head

Grab some **white poster board**, a **ruler**, and some **crayons**!

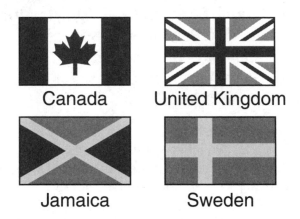

Lots of flags are symmetrical. Design your own flags. Each design should have at least one line of symmetry. Write a number next to each flag you draw. The number will show the number of lines of symmetry in your design. How many lines of symmetry can you make in a flag?

Cracking the Fourth Grade

Coordinate Grids

Coordinate grids might seem overwhelmingly complicated to a fourth grader. But a lot of kids have seen maps with coordinate grids—some may have even used maps to find a city or a street.

Although the term *coordinate grid* might be new to your fourth grader, a coordinate grid just allows your kid to locate a specific place by using numbered lines. Plotting coordinate points on a grid may seem abstract to your kid; your kid may feel it's just a lot of numbers and dots. Your kid may find that locating actual places on a grid is more concrete and makes more sense. Plotting locations on a grid is like using a map. Looking at grids and maps together can make it easier for kids to understand and visualize how coordinate grids work.

Encourage your child to think of practical uses for grids, such as finding a location on a map. He or she can see that finding the coordinates of a point on a grid is like following directions on a map. You can also use games to help him or her find coordinates and reinforce the importance of order when using coordinates.

First things first: Get a sense of what your kid already knows. Turn the page and tell your kid to Jump Right In!

Here's what you'll need for this lesson:
- paper
- pencil
- maps

Jump Right In!

Mya has to decide where she wants to go this weekend.

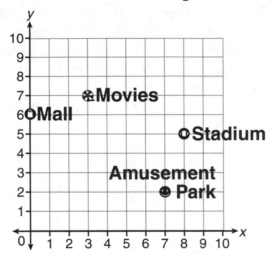

1. What are the coordinates of the movie theater?

   A. (0, 7)

   B. (3, 7)

   C. (7, 0)

   D. (7, 3)

2. What are the coordinates of the mall?

   A. (0, 6)

   B. (1, 6)

   C. (6, 0)

   D. (6, 1)

3. If Mya went to a place located at (7, 2), where did she go?

   A. amusement park

   B. mall

   C. movie theater

   D. stadium

Karen is drawing a map to show where she rides her bike every day after school. Answer questions 4 and 5 to get the locations.

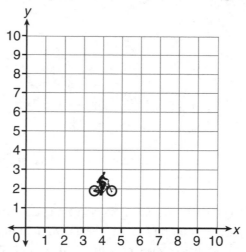

4. Karen rides to her friend's house located at (6, 4) on the grid. Place a point where Karen's friend's house is located on the grid above.

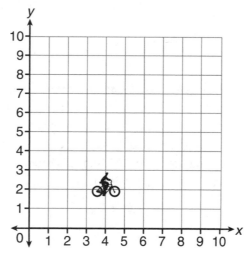

5. From her friend's house at (6, 4), Karen rides 2 units to the right and 3 units down to get to the library. What are the coordinates of the library?

Excellent Job!

 *Checking In*

Ⓐ Answers for pages 212 and 213:

    1. B

    2. A

    3. A

    4. An A+ answer: A point is placed at (6, 4).

    5. An A+ answer: The library is located at (8, 1).

Did your child get the correct answers? If so, you could give her new coordinates to plot on Karen's grid.

Did your kid get any of the answers wrong? If so, go over the incorrect answers. Ask, "What would you do to place a point on the grid?" Help your child remember the order of the coordinates. Tell him that just as x comes before y in the alphabet, the x-coordinate comes before the y-coordinate in a coordinate pair. Make sure he understands that he goes left or right (x-coordinate) and then up or down (y-coordinate) to find a location on the grid (and not the other way around).

 *Watch Out!*

If your kid is having a hard time using coordinate grids, you could draw a map of your neighborhood, your house, or your yard. Make sure it's on a grid and that the coordinates are numbers only or letters only but not both. Explain how the map is divided into squares. Set familiar locations on the map and ask your child to find their coordinates. Then, reverse the coordinates and have your kid find this other location. Reversing the coordinates helps your kid understand why the order of the coordinates is important.

What to Know...

Your kid will have to get these skills down in order to move forward in more advanced mathematics such as algebra and trigonometry. Also, the better she understands coordinate grids, the less chance she'll get lost (as long as she is wandering around with a map).

Review these skills with your child this way:

- A **coordinate grid** is a pattern of lines that cross each other—a plane in which a horizontal number line intersects a vertical number line at their zero points.

- An **ordered pair** is a pair of numbers that gives a location on a coordinate grid.

Your child can find places on a map that he or she may visit or places where relatives live.

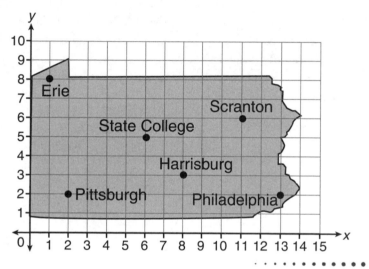

Encourage your child to find the coordinates of each of the cities on the map.

Mapmakers use a coordinate grid system to place locations on a map so that people will know the exact location of a city or a street and not get lost.

Encourage your kid to draw a map of his or her neighborhood on a grid. Ask the child what coordinates would locate your house.

 ## Checking In

Some kids struggle to see the relationship between the numbers on a coordinate grid. Use masking tape to make a coordinate grid on the floor (or chalk on outdoor concrete) and number the axes. Call out ordered pairs and have your child stand at each location on the grid. Occasionally reverse the ordered pairs and make sure the child knows the difference. Point out that when the order is reversed, the location is not the same.

Study Right

Throughout these activities, emphasize that the first number in a set of coordinates tells the number of units right from the origin (0, 0). In more advanced math, it will be right and left of the origin, with left being denoted by negative numbers. The second number in the ordered pair tells the number of units up from the origin. Later, negative numbers will represent movement down from the origin. Encourage your child to use his or her finger to track the number of units in each direction to avoid miscounting or other errors.

Fourth Graders Are...

Fourth graders like to search for things. Divide your home or yard into a "grid" and hide objects in each area. Give your kid coordinates and send him or her on a hunt to find those things!

On Your Way to an "A" Activities

{ **20** minutes }
Type: Game/Competitive
Materials needed: paper, pencil
Number of players: 2 or more

Play "Grid Battle." Each player makes a coordinate grid and places five points on the grid. Each point represents a warrior. The first player begins by calling the coordinates of a point and writing them on a piece of paper to keep track of the coordinates called. The opponent says whether it is a hit or miss—a hit defeats the warrior (if a warrior is at that coordinate). If it is a hit, place an X on that warrior. Players take turns calling out coordinates. The first player to defeat all of the opponent's warriors wins.

{ **20** minutes }
Type: Active
Materials needed: none
Number of players: 2 or more

Play "Movements in Space." Each player will find a space and map out a coordinate grid. A tiled area can help make mapping out a grid easier, but this can be done anywhere as long as whoever is playing knows how the grid is set up. Decide who is the first caller. This person will call out coordinates, and the other players will make movements (hop, dance, skip, etc.) to get to the place on the grid. The players then go back to the start, and another person will name coordinates. Each player will now use a different movement than they used in the last round to get to the new coordinates.

Has your child breezed through the activities? If so, he or she can work on this Using Your Head activity independently.

Using Your Head

*Grab some **paper** and a **pencil**!*

Draw a coordinate grid similar to the ones you have seen in this lesson. This grid will be a treasure map. Place treasures (by drawing symbols) at different locations on the map.

On the bottom of the paper, write the coordinates of each treasure. Then, write directions for a treasure hunter to easily locate each treasure.

Color or decorate your map as you wish.

Transformations

Transformations occur constantly around us. A chair is pulled from a table, the cap on a bottle is twisted open, a pancake is flipped; these are all examples of transformations. The term *transformation* is probably new to fourth graders and might sound intimidating because it's a mouthful. But your fourth grader has already had tons of experiences with transformations.

The term *transformation* refers to slides, turns, and flips. While these actions are part of everyday life, performing or identifying them on paper can be hard. Your kid has performed many real-life transformations, but he or she may not understand how to perform a slide, a turn, or a flip using two-dimensional shapes on a sheet of paper.

To help your kid better understand and perform transformations, you can demonstrate slides, flips, and turns using real-life objects and images in video games. You can also use paper cutouts to perform various transformations on pieces of paper and have your kid draw the original and the transformed image.

First things first: Get a sense of what your kid already knows. Turn the page and tell your kid to Jump Right In!

Here's what you'll need for this lesson:
- paper
- pencil
- construction paper
- fabric
- fabric glue
- scissors
- card stock
- crayons
- ruler

Carl is putting together a puzzle.

1. Which answer shows a slide of the puzzle piece?

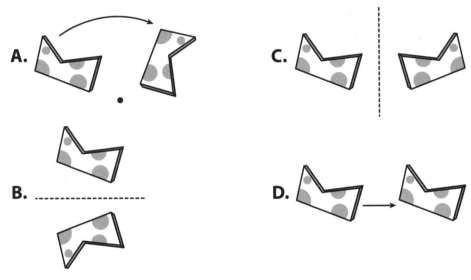

2. Which answer shows a turn of the puzzle piece?

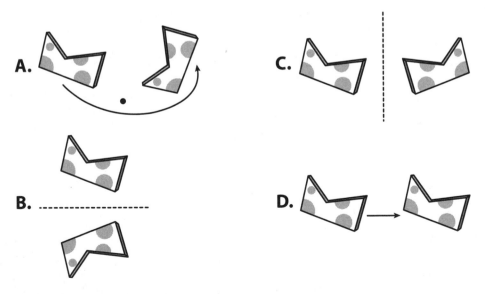

3. Which answer shows a flip of the puzzle piece?

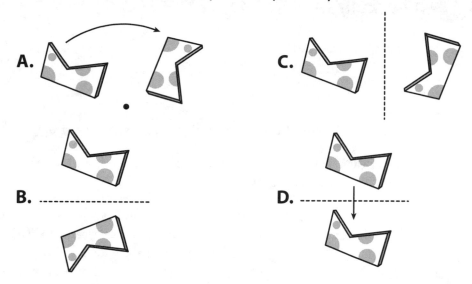

B. -

D. -

4. The shape below has to be flipped to fit into the right space in a video game. Draw a flip of this shape across the line.

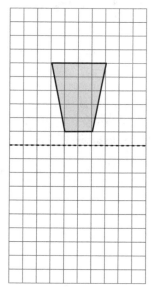

Excellent Job!

 **Checking In**

ⒶAnswers for pages 220 and 221:

> **1.** D
>
> **2.** A
>
> **3.** B
>
> **4.** An A+ answer: Shows a flip of the quadrilateral across the vertical line

Did your child get the correct answers? If so, you could have your kid identify the wrong answers as flips, slides, or turns.

Did your child get one of the answers wrong? Go over the incorrect answers with him. Ask, "How do you slide an object?" or "What is the difference between a turn and a flip?" Help him relate slides, flips, and turns to his own palms. Have your kid hold his palm in front of his face. Tell him to "slide" his palm up and down or from side to side, and make sure he notices that only the position has changed. Then, have him turn his palm and notice the differences in position. Finally, have your kid hold up his other palm, and explain that this is a flip (it looks like a mirror image). Have your kid explain the differences between the flip and the slide and the turn.

 **Watch Out!**

Throughout these activities, emphasize that the size and shape of an object does not change, but the position and the orientation may change. Children should compare some part of the original and the transformed figure to determine which transformation the shape has undergone.

What to Know...

Kids see and perform transformations constantly. Your child can benefit by becoming aware of the kinds of movements that he or she performs each day and by describing them as slides, flips, or turns.

Review these skills with your child this way:

- To **slide** a shape means to move it along a line.
- To **flip** a shape means to create a reflection of the shape on the opposite side of a line.
- To **turn** a shape means to move it around a point.
- A **line** is a straight path that goes in two directions and does not end.

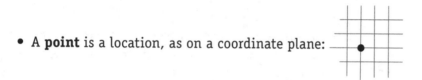

- A **point** is a location, as on a coordinate plane:

Your kid may see transformations in their surroundings, as with the car below.

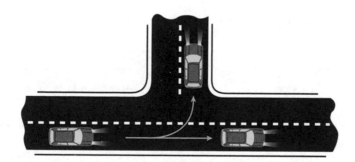

Have your child tell you the transformations that he or she sees in the picture. Ask your child how the car could show a flip, or use two toy cars to show these transformations.

Quilt makers transform shapes to make quilts.

Encourage your child to pick out slides, turns, and flips of the original colored triangles (to the left) within the quilt.

👉 Checking In

Some kids might not notice the differences between shapes that are turned, flipped, or slid. Use tracing paper to transform a shape. Have your child compare the different vertices and sides of the shape for each transformation (slide, flip, and turn). For each one, have your kid verbalize any difference between the original and the transformed shape. It's okay if he or she describes a flip as "backwards."

👍 Study Right

Some kids have trouble understanding how to transform a two-dimensional shape on paper. You can cut shapes from graph paper and spread them out (some should be identical). Have your child move the shapes from one spot to the next (for example, a shape may move down and then turn, or turn and then flip). Then, have her explain what kind of transformation she's just performed.

Fourth Graders Are...

Fourth graders like to make things and draw. Find some M.C. Escher art online and have your child decide how transformations are used for the art. Have your child create Escher-like art using transformations.

On Your Way to an "A" Activities

{20 minutes}

Type: Arts and Crafts
Materials needed: paper, fabric, scissors, fabric glue, construction paper
Number of players: 1 or more

Create a "Transformed Quilt." Cut a shape from paper to use as a pattern. Cut the shape from fabric, making sure that there are some flips of the shape. Glue the fabric shapes to a piece of construction paper. Be sure to include turns, slides, and flips of the shapes. You will have made a "quilt" that is a transformation of the paper pattern.

{40 minutes}

Type: Arts and Crafts
Materials needed: scissors, card stock, crayons, ruler, pencil
Number of players: 2 or more

Create a puzzle. Draw a picture on a piece of card stock or lightweight cardboard. Color the picture. Then, use a pencil and a ruler (for straight lines) to divide the picture into shapes—make sure you use turns, slides, and flips to create your shapes. Cut out each shape to get your puzzle pieces. Give the puzzle to someone to try to put together to recreate your picture.

Has your child breezed through the activities? If so, he or she can work on this Using Your Head activity independently.

Using Your Head

{ **45** minutes }

*Grab some **construction paper**, a **pencil**, some **paper**, and **scissors**!*

Draw each of the following on construction paper: a triangle, a rectangle, a pentagon, and a hexagon. For each shape, use slides, flips, and turns so that the shapes fit into one another without a gap and without overlapping. Here is an example of how you would use a triangle to do this.

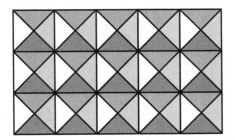

Now you try it!

How did you slide, flip, or turn the shape to make it fit?

Congruence and Similarity

Fourth graders see congruent and similar shapes everywhere. They see CDs or DVDs that are all exactly the same size and shape. They have their school photos taken and get the same picture in different sizes. These things show congruence and similarity. Although fourth graders have seen congruent and similar objects, they may not know or fully understand what this means because they don't commonly use these terms.

When students learn about *congruence*, they generally come to understand the term to mean "exactly the same." *Similarity* tends to be a bit more difficult, especially since they probably understand the word *similar* to mean "alike." In math, the term *similar* adds a new dimension to the idea of being alike, because in math two shapes need to have specific characteristics alike. This is a really difficult concept for kids to grasp.

Your fourth grader may have a hard time distinguishing when shapes are similar because their sizes vary. To help your kid better understand congruence and similarity, you can have him or her place one shape on top of another to see if they are congruent, or use different-sized leaves or cubes to help demonstrate similarity.

First things first: Get a sense of what your kid already knows. Turn the page and tell your kid to Jump Right In!

Here's what you'll need for this lesson:

- paper
- pencil
- construction paper
- photocopied pictures
- glue
- scissors
- index cards
- crayons
- ruler

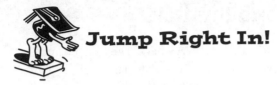 **Jump Right In!**

Kevin took a photo of his dog. Kevin's mom printed a few different sizes of the photo.

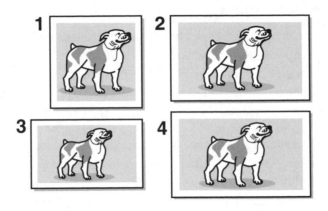

1. Which photos are congruent?

    A. 1 and 2

    B. 2 and 3

    C. 3 and 4

    D. 4 and 2

2. Which photos are similar?

    A. 1 and 2

    B. 1 and 4

    C. 3 and 1

    D. 4 and 3

The shape below will be used to make a quilt. Use the shape to answer questions 4 and 5.

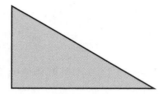

3. Some of the shapes in the quilt will be the same size and shape as the shape in the picture. Draw two shapes that are congruent to the shape in the picture.

4. Some of the shapes in the quilt will be the same shape but <u>not</u> the same size as the shape in the picture. Draw two shapes that are similar to the shape in the picture.

Excellent Job!

# Checking In

A Answers for pages 228 and 229:

1. D
2. D
3. An A+ answer: Two triangles that are exactly the same size and shape as the triangle in the picture
4. An A+ answer: Two triangles with the same angles as the one in the picture but either larger or smaller than the pictured triangle

Did your child get the correct answers? If so, you could ask, "How did you remember the difference between congruence and similarity?" Make sure your kid got the right answer because he or she knew the difference and wasn't just guessing.

Did your child get one of the answers wrong? If your kid got question 1 or 2 wrong, she may not remember the difference between "congruent" and "similar." If she got question 3 or 4 wrong, she may have a hard time recognizing similar and congruent shapes. Have your kid trace one shape on paper and cut it out, and then place this shape on top of the others to compare. Make sure she understands that congruent shapes are exactly the same size, that one should fit perfectly on top of the other, and that similar shapes have the same shape but may be different in size.

Fourth Graders Are...

Fourth graders like to collect things. Have your child collect leaves from a tree. Have the child place the leaves on top of one another to decide which are congruent and which are similar. Have your child talk about the qualities that make the leaves congruent or similar. They can then make a collage out of the leaves if they like.

What to Know...

Kids see congruent and similar shapes every day, although they may not think of them as congruent or similar.

Review these skills with your child this way:

- **Similar figures** are figures that have the same shape but are different sizes.
- **Congruent figures** are figures that have the same shape and size.

Your child sees congruent and similar shapes when you go shopping.

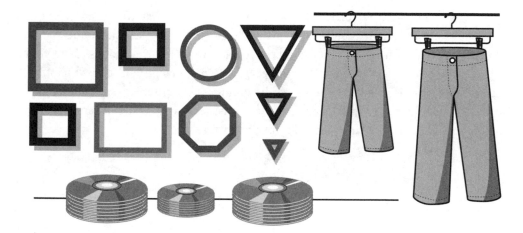

Encourage your child to color congruent shapes the same color. Ask her to color the similar circles blue, the similar squares yellow, and so on. Have your child identify congruent and similar shapes when you go shopping.

Study Right

Throughout these activities, make sure your child compares the sides and the vertices of the figures. They can color the parts of shapes to show the parts that are the same (or similar) when they compare two shapes. Stress that they should compare all parts before deciding whether a shape is congruent, similar, or neither.

Watch Out!

Some kids struggle with the difference between congruent and similar shapes. You can cut shapes from graph paper—some should be congruent, others should be similar, and others should be neither similar nor congruent. Spread out the shapes. Have your kid place shapes on top of one another to decide which are congruent and which are similar. Make sure he examines the shapes he groups as congruent to see that all sides and corners are the same. Then, make sure he notices that the corners of similar shapes are the same, but the length of the sides may be different.

On Your Way to an "A" Activities

Type: Arts and Crafts
Materials needed: black-and-white photocopied pictures (including enlarged and reduced copies), construction paper, scissors, glue, crayons
Number of players: 1 or more

Create a collage. Print black-and-white photocopies of the same picture—some should be the same size, some reduced in size, and some enlarged. Color the copies that show congruent images the same. Make sure you color each part of each congruent copy. Color the copies that are similar the same (but use a different color than the one you used for congruent copies). Make sure you color each part of each similar copy. Organize the copies to make a collage on construction paper. Glue the copies to the construction paper. Decorate the collage as you wish.

Type: Game/Competitive
Materials needed: index cards, paper, pencil
Number of players: 2 or more

Have a "Congruent/Similar Shapes" race. Write each of the following shapes on an index card: triangle, rectangle, pentagon, hexagon, octagon. The first player chooses an index card and shows it to the other players. Each player will draw that shape and then divide the shape so that the original is divided into congruent shapes. A player receives one point for each congruent shape into which the original is divided, and a player receives five bonus points if these shapes are similar to the original shape. Then, the next player takes a turn to choose a card that names a different shape.

Has your child breezed through the activities? If so, he or she can work on this Using Your Head activity independently.

Using Your Head

*Grab some **paper**, a **pencil**, a **ruler**, and some **crayons**!*

Design your own playground or play area. Use lots of shapes (both congruent and similar). Color all congruent triangles blue and all similar rectangles green. Pick out other colors to go with other shapes.

Patterns with Numbers and Shapes

Nature is bursting with patterns—like a spider's web, a peacock's feathers, or the stripes of a zebra. There are patterns in music, in our actions, and even the language we speak.

Math is a science of patterns. In school, children begin by learning patterns in colors, shapes, and numbers. They learn number patterns, often chanting as they skip-count— 2, 4, 6, 8 or 10, 20, 30, 40, and so on. They are taught to find patterns in order to solve problems, and later they'll continue to use patterns in algebra and advanced sciences.

In fourth grade, kids are expected to find and extend shape and number patterns, or to find a missing item in a pattern. In order to do this, they need to figure out the rules for those patterns. Sometimes kids who overgeneralize what they see may make mistakes with this. They may also be more familiar with patterns formed by adding numbers and may have difficulty when the rule requires that they subtract.

First things first: Get a sense of what your kid already knows. Turn the page and tell your kid to Jump Right In!

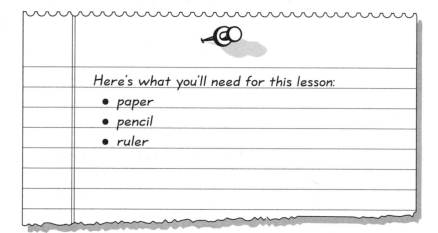

Here's what you'll need for this lesson:
- paper
- pencil
- ruler

Jump Right In!

1. Which shapes come next in the pattern below?

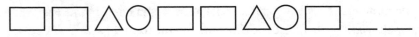

A. ▢ △

B. △ ◯

C. ▢ ◯

D. △ ▢

2. What is the next number in the pattern below?

20, 16, 12, 8, _____

A. 0

B. 4

C. 9

D. 10

3. What is the missing number in the pattern below?

38, 41, _____, 47, 50, 53

A. 42

B. 44

C. 46

D. 56

A sports store has several different displays set up.

4.

Write the rule for the pattern.

Draw the next shape in the pattern.

5.

Draw the pattern (but do not repeat the pattern).

Draw the next shape in the pattern.

Excellent Job!

Checking In

A Answers for pages 236 and 237:

1. A
2. B
3. B
4. An A+ answer: Child should write, "Bat, ball, ball, ball, hat." A drawing of a baseball bat.
5. An A+ answer: A drawing of 2 batons and a megaphone. For part 2, a baton.

Did your child get the correct answers? If so, you can ask, "How do you know what comes next in the pattern?" Have your kid identify the rule for each pattern, and make sure she got the right answer because she understood the pattern.

Did your child get one of the answers wrong? Go back over the incorrect answers. Ask, "Is the pattern getting bigger or smaller?" Or "How would you tell someone how to build this pattern?" Help your kid find a pattern that uses shapes by verbalizing the pattern in a rhythm (distinguishing between shapes)—for example, you could say, "star, star, big triangle, little triangle (pause) star, star, big triangle, little triangle." Then, have him decide what comes next or what is missing. For number patterns, ask if the numbers in the pattern are getting bigger or smaller. Help your kid understand that the only way a pattern can get bigger is to add to it or multiply, and the only way it can get smaller is to subtract from it or divide.

Watch Out!

Some fourth graders have a hard time identifying patterns. You can use objects around the house to make a pattern. Have your kid identify the pattern and then continue it. Then, make a pattern with missing objects in the middle. Have your child identify the number or object that completes the pattern. Make sure you include some patterns in which numbers are increasing and some in which numbers are decreasing.

What to Know...

Kids see and hear patterns every day, although they may not consciously take notice of these patterns. Your child can benefit by identifying patterns she sees or hears each day.

Review these skills with your child this way:

- A **pattern** is a series of numbers, figures, or pictures that follows a rule.
- A **rule** is a statement that tells how the items in a pattern are related.

Musicians repeat patterns of notes to make their music pleasing to the ear.

Have your child identify the pattern in this song: B, A, G, A; B, B, B. The placement of the notes on the G clef should help to show this pattern. Then, have her fill in the missing notes on the first and second lines. Encourage her to sing songs and identify the parts with patterns.

Checking In

Some kids have trouble recognizing and extending patterns. Use different kinds of patterns with your child. Make sure he notices whether the pattern repeats, increases, or decreases. If the pattern repeats, have him verbalize the pattern and then verbally continue the pattern. If the pattern increases, make sure he understands that something is added or multiplied. If the pattern decreases, then something is subtracted or divided. This strategy will help your kid narrow down what he needs to do to find the rule for a particular pattern. Once he knows the rule, he can extend the pattern or find missing item(s).

Have your child identify the rule for this pattern and fill in the missing number. Now, have him build patterns using addition and subtraction and things he sees. For example, he could build 1 pebble, 4 pebbles, 7 pebbles (rule: add 3).

Study Right

Throughout these activities, make sure your kid checks to make sure the pattern is consistent from one item to the next. Some kids might find a difference between the first two items and not check to make sure the rule works for all the other items. For example, if they subtract 2 to get the next number as in the example with the ducks, make sure that rule works for all the numbers in the pattern.

Fourth Graders Are...

Fourth graders are observant and like to mimic adults. As you perform activities each day, use some sort of pattern. Have your kid learn the pattern and then repeat it.

On Your Way to an "A" Activities

Type: Active
Materials needed: none
Number of players: 2 or more

Play follow the leader with "Pattern Noise." One player creates a pattern with a noise—clapping, stomping, and so on (or a combination of these). The other player has to repeat the pattern and then add to the pattern. Each player takes turns starting a pattern of noise.

Type: Speaking/Listening
Materials needed: none
Number of players: 1 or more

Find limerick patterns. Limericks are silly poems that have a certain pattern. Below is a limerick. First, say the limerick and think about the pattern. Then, replace the underlined words to make your own limerick. For example, you could begin by replacing <u>Charm</u> with <u>Peg</u> and then continue in the limerick pattern. Finally, try to come up with a different limerick that is all your own.

> There once was a lady named <u>Charm</u>
> Who accidentally broke her <u>arm</u>
> She slipped on the <u>ice</u>
> Not once, but <u>twice</u>
> Don't pity her, she came to no <u>harm</u>.

Has your child breezed through the activities? If so, he or she can work on this Using Your Head activity independently.

Using Your Head

{ 25 minutes }

*Grab some **paper**, a **pencil**, and a **ruler**!*

The puzzle below uses number patterns.

Here is an example you could start with, or you can come up with one of your very own. Draw a grid with four squares by four squares like the one below. You could have the numbers that run diagonally increase by 2, the numbers in the rows decrease by 1, and so on, until the entire grid is completed.

12	11	10	9
	14		
		16	
			18

Now, challenge your friends to figure out the number pattern that you created!

Answer: Line 2: 15, 14, 13, 12; Line 3: 18, 17, 16, 15; Line 4: 21, 20, 19, 18

Writing and Representing Equations

Fourth graders use equations in real-life situations, and it's helpful for them to think about equations as relationships, such as when they think of equal amounts, or compare sizes—for example, if person A is 2 inches taller than person B. As they learn more about relationships between numbers, they will start to see some of these situations as equations.

In fourth grade, your kid is expected to write and solve equations with unknown amounts and to write equations to solve word problems. Up until now, she has been asked only to perform operations on numbers to determine another number. Being asked to perform operations involving unknowns can be very abstract. The use of simple boxes to represent unknowns and to show that equations are balanced can help your kid better understand this concept. It's important for her to understand equations—they are one of the foundations of future study in algebra.

First things first: Get a sense of what your kid already knows. Turn the page and tell your kid to Jump Right In!

Here's what you'll need for this lesson:
- *paper*
- *pencil*
- *index cards*
- *balance*
- *hard-boiled eggs and 2 paper bags*

Jump Right In!

1. Jackie had 25 baseball cards. After her brother gave her some more cards, Jackie had 42 baseball cards. Which equation represents this?

   A. $25 + \boxed{} = 42$

   B. $\boxed{} = 42$

   C. $25 + 42 = \boxed{}$

   D. $\boxed{} = 25$

2. Which number should go into the box?

   $16 + \boxed{} = 18 + 12$

   A. 2

   B. 12

   C. 14

   D. 18

3. Which answer shows how to solve $3 \times \boxed{} = 45$?

   A. $3 + 45$

   B. 3×45

   C. $45 - 3$

   D. $45 \div 3$

4. Write a story problem for the equation $\boxed{} - 20 = 40$. Circle any clue words in the story that give information about the operation in the equation.

_____

_____

_____

_____

_____

_____

5. Solve the equation $\boxed{} - 20 = 40$.

_____

_____

_____

_____

Excellent Job!

 **Checking In**

ⓐAnswers for pages 244 and 245:

1. A

2. C

3. D

4. An A+ answer: Sample answer: "Jim gave 20 marbles to Jill. Jim had 40 marbles left. How many marbles did Jim have before he gave the marbles to Jill?" (*Gave* and *left* would be circled.)

5. An A+ answer:  = 60

Did your child get the correct answers? If so, you could ask, "How did you find the missing number?" Make sure your kid got the right answer because she understood how to do the problem. Then, have her build another equation.

Did your child get one of the answers wrong? Go over the incorrect answers with him. Ask, "What is the value on the left (or right) side of the equal sign? So what should be the value on the other side?" Make sure your kid understands that the box in the equation represents an unknown amount. Help him understand that the values on either side of the equal sign are the same. Label the left side of the equation *L* and the right side *R* so he will know what parts of the equation have the same value. Encourage him to simplify anything he can before trying to solve equations.

Watch Out!

If your kid is having difficulty solving equations, you can take her to the park and use a seesaw as an equation builder. Have two people about the same weight sit on each end of the seesaw. Have your kid write an equation to represent the situation. Then, place another person on one end. Ask your child what needs to happen to balance the seesaw. Have her write an equation to represent this situation. Repeat the process with different numbers of people on either end of the seesaw.

What to Know...

Kids use and solve equations all the time, even though they may not think about the fact that they are doing it.

Review these skills with your child this way:

- An **equation** is a mathematical statement that uses an equal sign (=). The values on either side of the equal sign are equal to each other.
- A **variable** is a symbol that represents an unknown value.

A landscaper may have to use unknowns to figure out the length of a fence he's building.

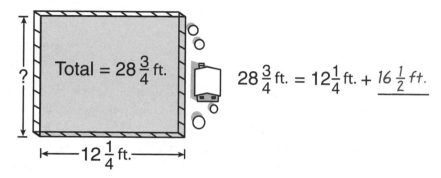

$$28\frac{3}{4} \text{ ft.} = 12\frac{1}{4} \text{ ft.} + \underline{16\frac{1}{2} \text{ ft.}}$$

A grocer may use and solve equations when he or she figures out how much of an item a person needs.

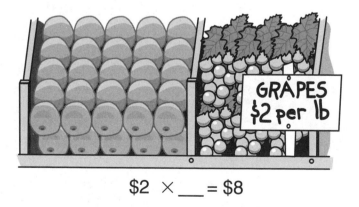

$$\$2 \times \underline{} = \$8$$

Encourage your child to write a word problem for the situation described in the picture and circle any key words in the problem that give clues as to which operation to use.

Checking In

Some kids struggle with equations no matter how hard they try. To help your child, you can have him practice writing equations for different situations and then solving the equations. For example, you could say, "Shaq wears number 32 in the game. Shaq's and D-Wade's numbers together make 35. What is D-Wade's number?" Point out key words like *together* to help children understand that this means addition. Have children come up with other words for addition, like *total*, *altogether*, and *sum*. Then, have them come up with words for other operations. Some of these words are as follows: *less than*, *minus*, *difference*, *left* for subtraction; *of*, *each*, *times*, *twice* for multiplication; and *shared equally* for division.

Study Right

As your kid learns to write and solve equations, make sure she reads word problems carefully and follows a problem-solving process (such as writing down what she knows and what she needs to find out). Have her circle words that give her clues as to which operation to use. Have your kid represent any unknowns with a box. She should first simplify any part of an equation that she can. Then, solve the equation. Have her write the number directly into the box that makes the equation true. This will help her understand that this number replaces the unknown.

Fourth Graders Are...

Fourth graders often like to go shopping. Take your child shopping, and have him or her bring along paper and a pencil. Have your child write and solve equations as you shop. For example, if bananas are 50 cents per pound, tell your child you want to spend $2.00 on bananas. Have him or her write and solve an equation to find the number of pounds of bananas you should get.

On Your Way to an "A" Activities

{25 minutes}

Type: Game/Competitive
Materials needed: index cards, paper, pencil
Number of players: 2 or more

Play "Equation Concentration." Write equations such as □ + 6 = 10 on one set of cards. Write solutions on another set of card (solutions can be numbers such as 4 or expressions such as 2 + 2).

Spread out the equation cards on the left side and the solution cards on the right. Each player takes turns picking up an equation card and a solution card to make matches. The player with the most matches wins the game.

{20 minutes}

Type: Reading/Writing
Materials needed: balance, hard-boiled eggs, paper, pencil, 2 brown paper bags
Number of players: 2 or more

One player places the same number of hard-boiled eggs in each of two brown paper bags (without the other player seeing the number of eggs in each bag). This player places both bags on the right side of the balance. The other player places eggs on the left side of the balance. Both players write an equation to represent this. Then, the player who is placing eggs on the left side has to write down the number of eggs in each bag. Repeat the process for a different number of eggs in the bags.

Next, place 4 eggs on each side of the balance. Remove 3 eggs from one side. Write down what you have to do to the other side to maintain the balance, and then try it. Replace all eggs. Add 2 more eggs to one side. Write down what you have to do to the other side to maintain the balance, and then try it.

Has your child breezed through the activities? If so, he or she can work on this Using Your Head activity independently.

Using Your Head

{ **15** minutes }

*Grab some **paper** and a **pencil**!*

Write an equation for the following situation (make sure you circle clue words that tell you which operation to use). Use ☐ to represent an unknown amount in the equation.

Together, a pack of gum and an apple cost the same amount as a granola bar and a fruit roll-up. The pack of gum is 25 cents, the apple is 60 cents, and the granola bar is 40 cents. How much is the fruit roll-up?

Solve the equation to solve the problem.

Answer: $.25 + $.60 = $.40 + [ ]; fruit roll-up = $.45.

Length and Weight

Kids measure things all the time. They stand back to back to see who's taller, they weigh themselves on a bathroom scale, or they compare how much things weigh by hand, saying that one thing is heavier than another. But kids might not measure things with measuring tools very often.

In the fourth grade, your kid is developing her measuring skills and is expected to use measuring tools with greater accuracy, as well as to know which units to use. She may sometimes make errors when measuring because she fails to align the zero end of the ruler with the end of the object she is measuring, and sometimes she may mix up the units of measurement.

To help your child use measuring tools and units correctly, you can give her lots of opportunities to measure the length and weight of a variety of objects. You can also help her to change one unit of measurement to another and recognize what units to use where.

First things first: Get a sense of what your kid already knows. Turn the page and tell your kid to Jump Right In!

Here's what you'll need for this lesson:
- *paper*
- *pencil*
- *index cards*
- *construction paper*
- *glue*
- *scissors*
- *ruler or tape measure*
- *scale*

Jump Right In!

1. What is the length of this candy cane (to the nearest half inch)?

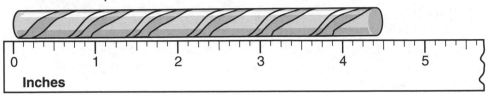

    A. 4 inches

    B. $4\frac{1}{2}$ inches

    C. 5 inches

    D. $5\frac{1}{2}$ inches

2. How much does this candy weigh?

    A. 0 pound

    B. 1 pound

    C. 2 pounds

    D. 3 pounds

3. Candies are sold by the number of ounces. A bag of candy is 2 pounds. How many ounces is this?

   A. 2 ounces

   B. 8 ounces

   C. 16 ounces

   D. 32 ounces

4. Tessa loves to hike, and this is the kind of shoe she has to wear when she's hiking.

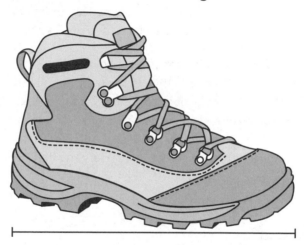

Use a centimeter ruler to find the measure of the shoe. (Hint: Because the line below the shoe is the same length as the shoe, you can measure the line to find out how long the shoe is!)

5. A football field is 100 yards long. How many feet long is the football field?

Excellent Job!

 *Checking In*

ⒶAnswers for pages 252 and 253:

  1. B

  2. D

  3. D

  4. An A+ answer: The shoe is 12.5 centimeters long.

  5. An A+ answer: The football field is 300 feet long.

Did your child get the correct answers? If so, you could ask, "In question 5, how did you convert yards into feet?" Or have her list all of the American units of length she knows as well as the metric units of length. Ask her where she's come across them before.

Did your child get one of the answers wrong? If so, go over the incorrect answers. For question 4, make sure your kid knows to line up the 0 on the rule with the left side of the object and then look at where the object ends on the right. Ask, "From what point do you begin your measurement and where do you end it?" If he has difficulty reading the ruler, show your kid the markers on a centimeter ruler as well as on a foot ruler. You can use tape to mark the ruler and write in quarter- and half-inches as well as half-centimeters.

 *Watch Out!*

Some kids struggle with measuring tools. You might have your child measure herself. Place your kid next to a wall and mark her height. Have her use a measuring tape to measure her height to the nearest inch, $\frac{1}{2}$ inch, and $\frac{1}{4}$ inch. Have your child convert the measurement from inches to feet—you can help her figure this out with the tape measure. Repeat the entire process using centimeters and meters. Next, set your kid on a bathroom scale, making sure she notices the scale is at zero first, and then how the needle moves as the scale is stepped on. Have her convert the number of pounds to ounces. Discuss why you might use one particular unit over another unit, like ounces instead of pounds or kilograms instead of grams.

What to Know...

People use measurements each day, as they may measure the length of a room or the height of a house. Or they may weigh food at a grocery store or weigh themselves on a scale at home. The more children measure real-life objects, the better they become at measuring.

Review these skills with your child this way:

- **Length** is the measure of the distance between two points.

- **Weight** is the measure of the heaviness of an object.

- The **American system of measurement** is a system of measurement commonly used in the United States. Inch, foot, and yard are units of length in the American system of measurement. Pounds and ounces are American units of weight.

- The **metric system of measurement** is a system of measurement used around the world. Centimeter and meter are units of length in the metric system of measurement. Grams and kilograms are metric units of weight.

A butcher has to weigh meat and cheese to be packaged.

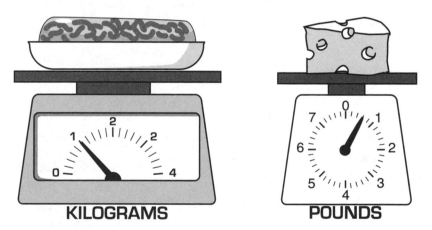

KILOGRAMS   **POUNDS**

Have your kid convert the measurements from the picture into different units: from pounds to ounces and from kilograms to grams. Choose objects from around the house for your kid to measure length and have him convert these measurements as well.

Have your kid get familiar with the different types of measurements within each system.

Metric Units	American Units
100 cm = 1 m	1 foot = 12 in.
1,000 mm = 1 m	1 yard = 3 ft.
1,000 g = 1 kg	1 mile = 5,280 ft.
1,000 mg = 1 g	16 ounces = 1 lb.

 *Checking In*

Estimating helps kids with measurements. Have your child identify an object that measures nearly 1 unit of measurement. For example, a baseball bat is about 1 meter, a strawberry is about 1 gram, a small paper clip is about 1 inch, etc. Have your kid find an object to use as a benchmark for her estimations of other objects' lengths and weights. After she's estimated with her reference, have your kid find the estimated item's exact length or weight. Refer to the definitions on page 255 to help her understand the two different systems of measurement. Make sure that she knows which units to use when measuring weight and which to use when measuring length.

 *Study Right*

Throughout these activities, emphasize accuracy. Point out that measuring to the nearest $\frac{1}{2}$ is more accurate than measuring to the nearest whole, and measuring to the nearest $\frac{1}{4}$ is more accurate than measuring to the nearest $\frac{1}{2}$, and so on.

Fourth Graders Are...

Fourth graders like to hunt for things. On separate pieces of paper, write out cm, m, g, kg, in., ft., yd., oz., and lb. and stick them in a hat. Have your kid pull out a piece of paper from the hat and find objects around the home that can be measured using each unit. Have your kid explain why this is the best unit of measurement to use for each object she brings back.

On Your Way to an "A" Activities

Type: Arts and Crafts
Materials needed: construction paper, glue, scissors, ruler
Number of players: 1 or more

Make measurement posters. Measure strips of construction paper one inch long. Form a design with the strips, and glue the design to a sheet of construction paper. Then, find pictures of objects that are about 1 inch long, and glue them to the bottom of the paper. This is an inch poster. Repeat the process for centimeter, feet, yard, and meter.

Type: Game/Competitive
Materials needed: index cards, paper, pencil
Number of players: 2 or more

Play "Go Fish" with measurement conversions. Write a whole unit measurement (for American or metric length or weight) on one card and its equivalent in another unit on another card (for example, 2 pounds on one card and 32 ounces on another). Shuffle the cards and give each player 7 cards. The rest of the cards stay in a pile. The players will put aside any matches from their hand that are equivalent. Then, the first player will ask for a card. If the second player has the card, he or she will give it to the first player, and the first player can ask for another card. If the second player does not have the card, then the first player will pick up a card from the pile. Then, the next player takes a turn to ask for a card. The game continues until one player runs out of cards. The person with the most correct matches wins the game.

Using Your Head

{ 25 }
minutes

*Grab a **pencil**!*

Write your estimate of the length or weight of each object shown below. Give your estimate in both American and metric units.

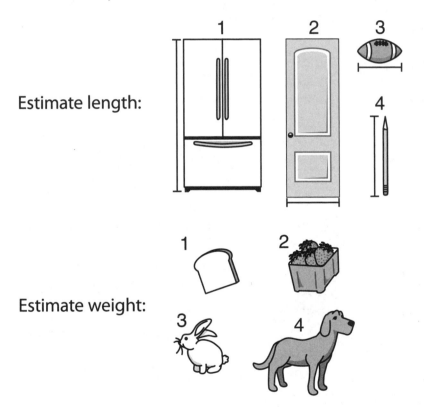

Estimate length:

Estimate weight:

Change each length or weight you wrote above to an equivalent measure using a different unit of measurement.

Answers: Length 1: 5 feet, 1.5 meters; 2: 3.5 feet, 1 meter; 3: 14 inches, 36 centimeters; 4: 8 inches, 20 centimeters. Weight 1: 2 ounces, 60 grams; 2: 1 pound, .5 kilograms; 3: 5 pounds, 2 kilograms; 4: 45 pounds, 20 kilograms.

Mean, Median, Mode, and Range

Data is all around us—on television, in newspapers, in magazines, and on the Internet. People collect all kinds of information, from the kinds of things people buy to information about the weather. They use graphs to organize and show the information visually, and analyze the graphs to make predictions.

In the fourth grade, kids are expected to gather data and organize it using different kinds of graphs. They are also expected to find the range, mean, median, and mode of data. They may find these measures of central tendency from graphs or from data sets. Kids generally do not use graphs in real life or find measures of central tendency, although they may hear about averages in sports like baseball, or with their grades in school.

To help your child organize and analyze data, you can give him or her opportunities to collect, display, and analyze real-life data, like temperatures or the time he or she spends watching television. You can show your kid how finding average amounts makes it easier to compare data or make predictions.

First things first: Get a sense of what your kid already knows. Turn the page and tell your kid to Jump Right In!

Here's what you'll need for this lesson:

- *paper*
- *pencil*
- *construction paper*
- *glue*
- *scissors*
- *crayons*
- *newspapers/ magazines*

Jump Right In!

The chart below shows the temperatures for one week in the city where Mike lives.

Mon.	Tues.	Wed.	Thurs.	Fri.	Sat.	Sun.
52°	55°	50°	55°	60°	60°	60°

1. What is the median of the temperatures shown for this week?

   A. 55°F

   B. 52°F

   C. 60°F

   D. 10°F

2. What is the mode of the temperatures shown in the chart?

   A. 8°F

   B. 55°F

   C. 56°F

   D. 60°F

3. What is the range of the temperatures shown in the chart?

   A. 10°F

   B. 50°F

   C. 55°F

   D. 60°F

Tyra is having a party. She wants to have her friends' favorite foods at the party, so she did a survey and made the table below.

Favorite Food	Number of Friends
Hamburger	6
Hot Dog	2
Pizza	10
Spaghetti	10
Taco	8

4. Show the data in the table in the pictograph below.

Favorite Food	Number of Friends	Key
Hamburger		
Hot Dog		
Pizza		
Spaghetti		
Taco		

each = 2 friends

5. What is the mean of the data in the table?

Excellent Job!

Checking In

Answers for pages 260 and 261:

1. A
2. D
3. A
4. An A+ answer: The pictograph should contain 3 hamburgers, 1 hot dog, 5 pizzas, 5 spaghettis, and 4 tacos.
5. An A+ answer: The mean is 7.2.

Did your child get the correct answers? If so, you could ask, "What did you do to get your answer?" Make sure she got the right answer because she understood how to make sense of the data given and wasn't guessing.

Did your child get one of the answers wrong? If so, go over the incorrect answers. Ask, "How do you find the mode (median, range, or mean)?" Or "What does the height of the bars on a bar graph tell you?" Help your child remember the difference between mode, median, and mean by telling him that he can think of **mo** in **mo**de as standing for the number that occurs **mo**st often. The median is in the middle of the road, so it is the middle number in a data set (and "median" also sounds similar to "middle"). Help your child understand that when we speak of averages in real life, we almost always refer to the mean.

Watch Out!

Some kids have a hard time creating graphs or representing data with averages. Draw a vertical and horizontal line on a large piece of construction paper and label the horizontal axis with the days of the week and the vertical axis with numbers. Each day, have your child mark the number of hours he or she watches television (or plays music or practices soccer). At the end of two weeks, have your kid color in the bars. Help your kid find the mean, mode, median, and range of this data.

What to Know...

People use graphs and measures of central tendency to organize information and use this information to make predictions.

Review these skills with your child this way:

- A **tally** is a way of counting by making a mark for each item counted.
- A **tally chart** is a table that shows data with tally marks.
- A **pictograph** is a graph that shows data by using picture symbols. Each pictograph has a key that tells how many items each symbol represents.
- A **bar graph** is a graph that shows data by using bars of different sizes.
- The **mean** is the average of the numbers in a set of data. The mean is calculated by adding the numbers in a set of data and then dividing by the number of items of data.
- The **median** is the middle number in a set of data when the data is ordered from least to greatest. If there is an even number of items of data in a set, the median is the mean of the two middle numbers.
- The **mode** is the number(s) or item(s) that occurs the most often in a set of data.
- The **range** is the difference between the least and greatest numbers in a set of data.

Your kid might keep a tally chart of the number of baseball cards he has of different players. He might look at data about sports and professional athletes as well.

Player	# of cards
R. J.	|||
F. R.		
M. S.	₩
K. G.	₩ ||||
D. W.	₩	

Player	At Bats	Hits
Reggie Jackson	9,864	2,584
Frank Robinson	10,006	2,943
Mike Schmidt	8,352	2,234
Ken Griffey	8,298	2,412
Dave Winfield	11,003	3,110

Your child could determine how batting average is calculated for these stats by dividing the number of at-bats of a player's career by the number of total hits he had. Encourage your child to use a calculator to determine the players' averages.

Have your child figure out the mean, median, mode, and range of hits for these five players.

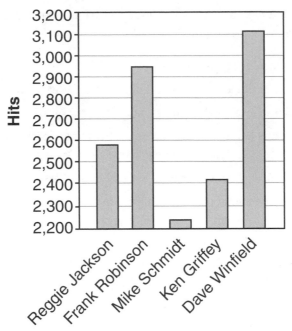

Study Right

When children are finding the mean, median, mode, and range, they need to list the data from least to greatest. When they have arranged the data from least to greatest, have them count to confirm that they have included all the data from the set.

Checking In

Kids can easily make mistakes when organizing information in graphs or finding the mean, median, mode, or range. They may focus on the graph itself, rather than the information it contains. For example, a pictograph showing information about children's favorite ice-cream flavors may have a key showing that 1 picture of an ice-cream cone = 2 children. The bar on the graph for chocolate shows 4 ice-cream cones (8 children). When asked about how many children picked chocolate, a child may respond that 4 kids picked chocolate. Help your kid avoid this kind of mistake by helping her notice all the elements of a graph that are important. Whenever you and your child create or analyze a graph, make sure you look at the labels, scales, and keys. Have your child underline or circle key elements of the graph that she needs to take into consideration.

On Your Way to an "A" Activities

{ 25 minutes }

Type: Reading/Writing
Materials needed: newspapers/magazines, construction paper, paper, pencil, scissors, glue
Number of players: 1 or more

Find graphs or charts with information from the newspaper or magazines. Write down what the graph or chart is about. Then, write a list of all the data you see. Order the data from least to greatest. Find the mean, median, mode, and range of the data. Cut out each graph or chart and glue it to construction paper. Write the mean, median, mode, and range under each chart or graph. You can start to collect information about topics (like sports or weather) that you are interested in and keep a log book.

{ 20 minutes }

Type: Reading/Writing
Materials needed: construction paper, paper, pencil, crayons
Number of players: 1 or more

Make your own survey! You might ask, "Which of these is your favorite ice-cream flavor?" Ask a number of different people and record their responses. Organize the responses in graphs on construction paper. Color the graphs.

Fourth Graders Are...

Fourth graders like to look at pictures and figure out what things mean. Have them look at graphs or charts you find on the Internet or in magazines or books. Ask them, "What kind of information is in this graph (or chart)?"

Has your child breezed through the activities? If so, he or she can work on this Using Your Head activity independently.

Using Your Head

{20 minutes}

Grab a pencil!

Mon.	Tues.	Wed.	Thurs.	Fri.	Sat.	Sun.
75°	80°	80°	70°	75°	75°	70°
0 in. rain	2 in. rain	1 in. rain	2 in. rain	0 in. rain	1 in. rain	1 in. rain

Create a graph or graphs to show the information about the temperatures or the rainfall above.

Find the mean, mode, median, and range of the information in your graph.

Answers: Mean, mode, and median temperature is 75 degrees. Range is 10 degrees. Mean, mode, and median rainfall is 1 inch. Range is 2 inches.

Perimeter and Area

You want to teach your children that what they learn in school is important. But sometimes when your kid asks, "Why do I have to do this?" it's hard to come up with a good answer.

Your kid might ask, "Why do I have to learn area formulas?" You might come up with a fairly routine response: "Because you'll use it in real life." Sometimes this is enough to keep your kid excited and interested. But a lot of the time, your child's eyes will glaze over and he'll turn away. When, how, and why your child could use it in real life—that's the stuff he really needs to hear.

Unfortunately, your kid uses this knowledge mainly in math class and on tests, and he probably has to answer questions about topics he finds boring. Now is the time to get your kid measuring perimeter and area at home with stuff he finds fun and exciting. Video games, building tree houses, arts-and-crafts projects, making gifts, or anything that brings these skills out of the classroom and into your kid's actual life will probably increase his interest in the subject. And these are all things he couldn't do when he was smaller, but he can work with now. So, not only will you be helping your child with math skills, you'll be helping him realize that he's growing up.

First things first: Get a sense of what your kid already knows. Turn the page and tell your kid to Jump Right In!

Here's what you'll need for this lesson:
- paper
- markers or crayons
- pencils
- 12 index cards

Jump Right In!

1. The school track team wants to run for 200 yards. Which of the following paths could they follow to run 200 yards?

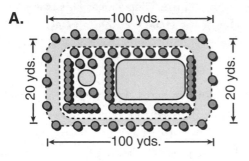

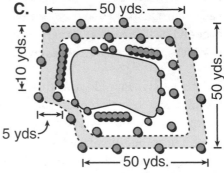

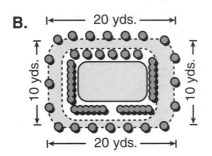

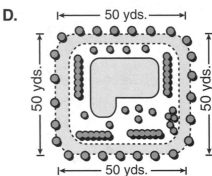

2. A local boat club wants to make a flag to hang from their boat. The base of the triangle has to be 6 feet, and the height has to be 7 feet. How many square feet of fabric will they need to make this flag?

   A. 42 square feet

   B. 26 square feet

   C. 21 square feet

   D. 13 square feet

Ray and Tabby made plans to build a tree house.

3. Ray plans to put a piece of rope around the box so he can load up supplies and bring them into the tree house. How long should the rope be to go around the box?

4. Tabby plans to build the door. How many square meters of wood will she need to use to build the door?

 ## Checking In

Ⓐ Answers for pages 268 and 269:

    1. D

    2. C

    3. An A+ answer: "The rope needs to be at least 10 meters long."

    4. An A+ answer: "Tabby will use 2 square meters of wood."

Did your child get the correct answers? If so, ask how. You could say, "Did you find the correct answer using the formula or using another method?" Make sure your child got the right answer because he or she knew the skills (and didn't guess).

Did your child get one of the answers wrong? If so, go over the incorrect answers. Ask, "What did you do to get that answer?" Ask, "Is this question asking you to find the measure of a distance around a shape (perimeter) or the amount of space covered by a shape (area)?" Help your child remember the difference between perimeter and area with this memory tip, "You can measure peri**meter** in **meters**, inches, yards, and other units. But you have to measure area in square meters, square inches, etc."

 ## Watch Out!

Sometimes fourth graders mix up the concepts of area and perimeter. Did your child find the area for question 3 (instead of the perimeter) or the perimeter for question 4 (instead of the area)? If so, your kid needs a reminder.

Find a book and trace it on paper to show your kid the perimeter of the book cover. Then, cut a piece of paper the same size as the book cover to show the area of the book cover.

What to Know...

Kids use perimeter and area all the time in everyday life.

Review these skills with your child this way:

- **Perimeter** is the measure of the distance around a two-dimensional shape. To find the perimeter, you can add together the lengths of all the sides of the shape.

- **Area** is the amount of space inside a two-dimensional shape. **Square units** are used to express area. To find the area of a shape, use a formula.

Your child could find the perimeter of a gift box using a ribbon.

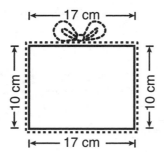

· · · · · · · · · · · · ·

Ask your child to use a tape measure to find the perimeter of her room, the board for a board game, etc.

An artist or architect might find the area of a shape on a grid by counting square units. Your child might have seen this done by people using maps.

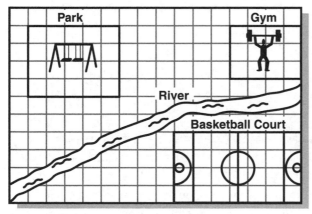

Area of a basketball court = 28 square units

· · · · · · · · · · · · ·

Encourage your child to count the units of the basketball court aloud. As your child counts a unit, he or she should draw a small dot in the unit with a pencil to show that it has already been counted.

You might find the area of a room when buying a rug.

square	$A = (s)(s)$	**Living Room**	side = 3 yards	$A = (3 \text{ yards})(3 \text{ yards})$ $A = 9$ square yards
rectangle	$A = l \times w$	**Hallway**	length = 2 meters width = 4 meters	$A = (2 \text{ m})(4 \text{ m})$ $A = 8$ square meters
triangle	$A = \frac{1}{2}(b)(h)$	**Playroom**	6 ft. 8 ft.	$A = \frac{1}{2}(8 \text{ ft.})(6 \text{ ft.})$ $A = \frac{1}{2}(48 \text{ square feet})$ $A = 24$ square feet

 ## Checking In

Is your kid forgetting the formulas? Cut a square-shaped piece of paper. In the center of the paper, tell your child to write "Area of a square = $(s)(s)$. Then, fold the paper in half to form two triangles. Open the paper. On the blank side, tell your child to write "Area of a triangle = $\frac{1}{2}(b)(h)$" in the center of each triangle. Explain that the area of each triangle is half the area of the square, and so the area formula for a triangle is half the area formula for the square.

 ## Study Right

Your child should clearly label diagrams. Remind him by showing him how. If you ever have to make a diagram, label it so your kid sees you using this study skill. It never hurts to practice what you preach. If your child needs to draw and measure a shape in the activities or in school work, check that he includes labels. Clear labels tell the measurement and the unit. This can help your child avoid simple errors.

Fourth Graders Are...

There's a pretty good chance that your child loves tools. Playing around with rulers and calculators can be a lot of fun for fourth graders. Give your kid lots of time to practice. The more time she works at these skills with the tools she needs, the better she'll get.

On Your Way to an "A" Activities

{ 10 minutes } Type: Game/Competitive
Materials needed: none
Number of players: 2 or more

Play "20 Questions" about perimeter. Think of an everyday thing that "goes around" a shape and shows its perimeter, such as a a gift ribbon (perimeter of a gift box), a rubber band, a picture frame (perimeter of a picture), and so on. Now, have your parent or friend ask 20 "yes or no" questions about this thing that shows perimeter. Once your parent or friend guesses it correctly, switch turns. Now, your parent or friend should think of an everyday thing that shows perimeter. You should ask 20 "yes or no" questions to identify that thing. See how many things you can identify!

{ 20 minutes } Type: Game/Competitive
Materials needed: 12 index cards, rulers, pencils
Number of players: 2 or more

Play a game of "Area Memory." Write the word "Area" on 6 index cards. Draw a square on two of those cards below the word "Area." Draw a rectangle on two of the cards and a triangle on two of the cards in the same way. On the other 6 index cards, write the formulas for the area of a square, rectangle, and triangle. Write each formula on two cards.

Shuffle the cards and place them facedown. Now, take turns with your parent or friend picking a pair of cards. If you find a correct pair, then you can keep the cards. If not, you must return them facedown. Keep playing until all the cards have been correctly paired.

Has your child breezed through the activities? If so, he or she can work on this Using Your Head activity independently.

Using Your Head

{ **25** minutes }

*Grab some **paper, pencils,** and **crayons** or **markers**!*

Count the number of units along the sides of the squares and rectangles to find their perimeters. Color shapes with a perimeter of 8.

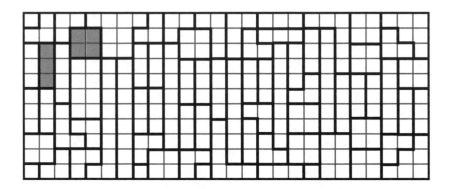

Count the number of units in the shapes to find their areas, or use a formula. Color all the shapes with an area of 10 or 4.

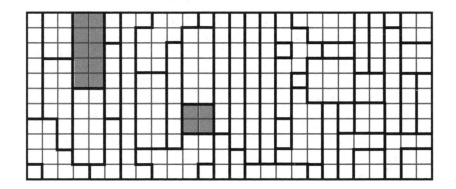

Answer: The colored squares and rectangles say Good Job!

Probability

Probability is all about chance. Kids see probability in action when they flip a coin to see who goes first in a game or when they hear a weather forecaster predict the chance of rain.

In fourth grade, kids are expected to understand whether events are *certain, likely, unlikely,* or *impossible* to happen. They need to understand the precise nature of these terms as they are used in math. Kids sometimes choose whether something is *likely* or *unlikely* based solely on their preferences, rather than on data. For math questions, this won't fly. They need to base their decisions on the data given and not on their feelings.

Some things that could help with probability, like playing cards, aren't always used in the classroom, since they are associated with gambling. Dice have a more politically correct name—your kid may have heard his teacher calling them "number cubes." You can certainly use cards and dice at home, as well as coins, to help kids understand probability.

First things first: Get a sense of what your kid already knows. Turn the page and tell your kid to Jump Right In!

Here's what you'll need for this lesson:
- *paper*
- *pencil*
- *construction paper*
- *deck of cards*
- *index cards*
- *coin*

Jump Right In!

1. If a coin is flipped, it is _____ to get either heads or tails.

   A. certain

   B. impossible

   C. likely

   D. unlikely

2. If Dante picks a baseball cap without looking, it is _____ that he will pick the red cap.

   A. certain

   B. impossible

   C. likely

   D. unlikely

3. What is the probability of getting heads when a coin is flipped?

   A. $\dfrac{1}{3}$ **C.** $\dfrac{1}{1}$

   B. $\dfrac{1}{2}$ **D.** $\dfrac{2}{1}$

Joan, David, Lucille, Mindy, and Tyrone decided to be teammates to play basketball. Answer questions 4 and 5 about the team.

4. The team needs a captain. If they all put their names in a box and one name is pulled out without looking, what is the probability that the captain will be a girl?

5. One person is chosen at random to bring snacks for the next game. What is the probability that Lucille is chosen to bring snacks for the next game?

Excellent Job!

 *Checking In*

Ⓐ Answers for pages 276 and 277:

1. A

2. D

3. B

4. An A+ answer: The probability that the captain will be a girl is $\frac{3}{5}$.

5. An A+ answer: The probability that Lucille is chosen to bring snacks for the next game is $\frac{1}{5}$.

Did your child get the correct answers? If so, you could ask, "How did you find the probability?" Have your kid walk you through the process she used to figure out the answer to make sure she understands the concept.

Did your child get one of the answers wrong? If so, go over the incorrect answers. Ask, "How do you figure out all the possible choices?" Make sure your kid understands that the probability is the number of favorable outcomes over the total number of possible outcomes. If an event is certain, then every single outcome is favorable; if an event is impossible, then there are absolutely no favorable outcomes.

 *Watch Out!*

Some kids really struggle with understanding probability. Grab a number of baseball caps (or socks)—some should be the same color, others different colors. Show your child that if you wanted to pick a color that is not there, then it is *impossible* to pick that color. Then, show your child that if he had a group of socks that were all white, then it would be *certain* that he would randomly choose a white sock from that group of socks.

What to Know...

Lots of people refer to probability every day: from stockbrokers to weather forecasters and mathematicians to picnickers. For example, if the weather forecaster reports that it is *likely* to rain on July 4th, you may not plan a picnic on that day.

Review this skill with your child this way:

- **Probability** is the likelihood that an event will happen. Probability is shown as a number from 0 to 1.

Weather forecasters use probability to predict the weather. Your kid may have heard a forecast similar to this one:

On Tuesday July 3rd, there is a 3 out of 4 chance of rain. If you're going anywhere, you might want to bring an umbrella.

· · · · · · · · · · · · · · · · · · · ·
Have your child represent the possibility of rain on July 3rd as a fraction.

Some games require that you use a spinner to figure out your next move.

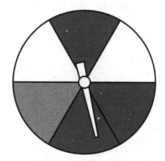

Ask your child to figure out the probability of the spinner landing on a red section. Have your child use *certain*, *likely*, *unlikely*, or *impossible* to describe the possibility of landing on a section of the spinner. For example, it is impossible to land on a green section, but it is likely to land on a red one.

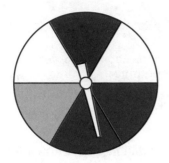

Show your kid that he can represent the probability of landing on a red section as a fraction by taking the number of red sections in the spinner and placing this number over the total number of sections in the spinner.

 ## Checking In

Kids can easily make mistakes when finding probabilities. Make sure your child is able to grasp the meaning of favorable outcomes as well as total outcomes. In the classroom, she is expected to use fractions to show probabilities. Because this is an unfamiliar concept, she may place the number of chances for a certain outcome in the denominator instead of the numerator. Children may also run into trouble while determining the number of chances for a certain outcome and the total number of possible outcomes. Emphasize that the outcomes must be based on data and not on preference. Show her that the total number of outcomes is always in the denominator of the fraction. Point out that a probability cannot be less than 0 or greater than 1.

 ## Study Right

Throughout these activities, emphasize how to write a probability as a fraction. Have the child write down the formula as follows, and then refer to it each time he or she writes a probability as a fraction.

$$\frac{Favorable\ outcomes}{Possible\ outcomes}$$

Fourth Graders Are...

Fourth graders like to experiment and make predictions. Have your child decide on the probability of getting heads (or tails) when he flips a coin. Then, have him flip a coin 100 times to see how many heads (or tails) he gets. Make sure your child puts a tally mark to record each one. Then, ask your kid what is the actual probability he found for getting heads (or tails). Ask your child, "The next time you have to flip a coin to see if you go first in a game, what side will you choose?"

On Your Way to an "A" Activities

{ 25 minutes }
Type: Game/Competitive
Materials needed: deck of cards, paper, pencil
Number of players: 2 or more

Play "Cards of Chance." The first player will name a criterion for choosing a card (for example, a card from a black suit). Then, the second player states the probability (he or she can look through the cards to decide on the probability). The player gets 1 point for stating the correct probability. The cards are then shuffled, and the player chooses a card. The player gets another 5 points if the card selected fits the criterion stated. The card is replaced, and the next person takes a turn. The player with the most points at the end of the game wins.

{ 15 minutes }
Type: Game/Competitive
Materials needed: index cards, construction paper, scissors
Number of players: 2 or more

Play "Deal Me." Draw a pig on one index card, a deflated balloon on another, and a car on another (or glue on a picture of each). Then, cut 3 large square pieces of construction paper and number them 1, 2, and 3. The dealer will place an index card under each numbered card without letting the other player see. Then, ask the player to choose a numbered card. The dealer will ask, "Would you like to switch to card 2 (for example)?" If yes, the player will answer, "Deal me," and if not, "No way." Then, the dealer flips the card the player selects to see if the player wins the car. The roles are then reversed. At the end of the game, explain the probability of finding the car. Explain whether the probability changes the more times the car is located.

Has your child breezed through the activities? If so, he or she can work on this Using Your Head activity independently.

Using Your Head

$\left\{ \begin{array}{c} \textbf{30} \\ \textbf{minutes} \end{array} \right\}$

*Grab a deck of 52 **playing cards**!*

What is the probability of picking a 3 without looking?

What is the probability of picking a card that is <u>not</u> a face card (Jack, Queen, King)?

Explain which is greater—the probability of picking a face card (Jack, Queen, King) or the probability of picking a spade.

Answers: 4 out of 52. 40 out of 52. Picking a spade is slightly more probable.

282   Cracking the Fourth Grade

Success in School Begins at Home

A new series from The Princeton Review that informs parents and helps children succeed through hands-on lessons and exercises

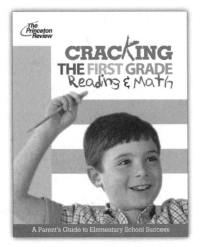

Cracking the First Grade
ISBN: 978-0-375-76602-2

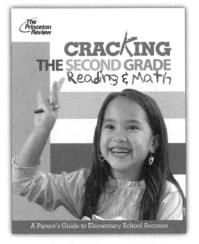

Cracking the Second Grade
ISBN: 978-0-375-76603-9

Cracking the Third Grade
ISBN: 978-0-375-76604-6

Cracking the Fourth Grade
ISBN: 978-0-375-76605-3

$14.95/$16.95 CAN. | Trade Paperback | 7 x 9 in.